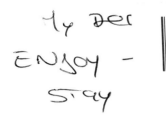

# Healing Letters

## By
## Aurea Reis

# Healing Letters

Authored by Aurea Reis
© Aurea Reis 2020
Cover Illustrator Samantha Spence

Edited by Marcia M Publishing House Editorial Team Published by Marcia M Spence of Marcia M Publishing House, West Bromwich, West Midlands the UNITED KINGDOM B71

**MARCIA M**
PUBLISHING HOUSE

# Dedications

**To my mom:** My Life begins with and from you. Our road to healing has been long and painful, but, in that journey, I managed to absorb your resilience, your work ethics, your moral values and your Kind Heart. I now understand you and respect your life story, and I have never been prouder of the woman you are. I am forever grateful to the Above to have to give me you as my mother. You are and always will be my role model and my All. Thank you for having me, thank you for raising me, thank you for holding me in difficult times and thank you for loving me unconditionally. You are my Queen, my 'Home', and I Love you beyond words. When I 'grow up' I hope to be half of the woman that you are.

**To my son:** Life started to make sense from the minute that you were born. God knew I needed you in my life. I was a lost soul, and you put meaning into it all. Your innocent and unprotected being forced me to want to be better for you and for myself. Every day I try to keep it in mind. Thank you for teaching me how to Love unconditionally, thank you for making me work tirelessly to be a better human being, thank you for all the kisses and hugs (they are my oxygen), thank you for just being my son, my beautiful Angel, my present of God. Most of all, Thank you for keeping me alive when the sky was dark, and my soul was numb. I love you, I love you, I love you… to the infinite and back.

**To my friend, Elisabete:** Ah, my dear, my life would not be the same without you. You are the true meaning of the word 'friend.' My biggest cheerleader and soul mate. You loved me through my 'ugly' days without judgements. You didn't know my 'true' story, but you remained close and loyal. You created a safe space 'free of expectations, and consequently, our hearts aligned perfectly. You were the first to read this book and to push me to have it published. Your enthusiasm, your genuine happiness for everything I do, have, or represent makes me sometimes wonder, what I have done to deserve a loyal and loving friend like you. I promise never to disappoint you, always have your back, and continuously love you beyond your crankiness and bossy ways (laughs). I believe that our friendship comes from another life and I am sure to follow to the next one. A love like ours cannot be resumed to exist only in this life. You are no doubt one of my favourite human beings, and that is why I chose you to be my (our) son's Godmother. Thank You for 'Seeing' me when no one else did. My BB, I love you endlessly.


**To You:** You that cry in silence when friends misjudge you or do not understand you. You that carry deep secrets that hunt you day and night. You that have a love for your children but fail to know how to put it out to them. You that love your family but need them to 'see' you and not constantly fight you. You that learned to fight at a young age and continue to do so even when not required. You that are hurting from your traumas but are scared to address them. You that were bullied and become resentful. You that want to be loved but fail to love yourself first. You that seek a partner but always end up hurting. You that want to tell your truth to the world but are afraid to be judge and victimised. You that are tired of being angry, miserable, depressed and in pilot mode. You that felt unloved and uncared for so long.

I hope this book gives you the strength to say enough, not just to others but to yourself. Everything begins and ends with You. Seek healing and forgiveness for you and not for others. Understand your story, look yourself in the mirror, unleash your demons, look them in the eyes, talk to them and if they do not want to listen then write them down. When you do so, address the hurt and the pain but also the learning experience. What did that experience, and moment teach you? For sure, your resilience, your strength and your character have come from those experiences. They might not have been fun, but you survived. You are not that unprotected child with no voice anymore. Seek help (therapy), talk your demons to trusty ears, and trust the people who love you with your 'Ugly'. Put your 'Walls' down, stop fighting (not everything is a war) and learn to be vulnerable.

Stop doubting your greatness as a mother, as a daughter, as a friend and as a lover. Start seeing yourself through the eyes of those that genuinely love you and you will 'See' what they saw all along… Not a perfect human being but a human deserving of love and affection. A human capable of love beyond comprehension if only You let 'Go' of everything that takes you away from your purpose in life. Understand Them (the people that hurt you), forgive them, forgive you (for allowing them that liberty, for feeling guilty or deserving of it all) and let them 'Go' (if you need to).

You that now found your voice and your peace of mind. You that learned to forgive yourself and others. You that accept love without questioning your right for it. You that talk and give love. You that work tirelessly to be the best parent and human being you can be. You that walk on purpose and listens to God calls. I write this book to YOU as you are ME!

# Acknowledgements

Although this is my memoir and my journey through healing, I cannot dismiss the few people who have been there for me or have influenced me in a way. It would be selfish of me to ignore their importance and impact on my life. Therefore, I will take this space to do my acknowledgements:

**To my family:** Through writing this book, I gained more love and respect for my family. Me and my sisters are so different but so equal, and now that they have read the book, we managed to put our difference asides. Although my Dad is still an enigma to me, I love him and respect him as such. My family and I have been estranged most of my life, but now we laugh and address each other with love, and I feel very much blessed to have you in my life. I feared your reaction after reading the book, but you surprised me with your support, which means a lot.

**To my support network around my son:** I often say that I am not a single mother because I have you all behind me. A group of strong women/men supporting and helping me with the most precious thing in my life. You make my life easy so many times and that helped me through difficult times and still do. Thank you for your constant help Shaveta & Padreep, Tania, Catarina & Nilton, Marisa, Catia & Daniel, Marlene & Raimond, Ju, Vania & Rui. My son feels safe around you, and that is all I need/needed at certain moments. A safe place for him to go so I could/can rest and reset.

**To my long-life Friends:** Tany, Silo, Dino, Beto, Carlinha, Vanda, Vania, Samira, Milene, Angelina, Marilia, Herica, Leila, Solange, Zuraima, Wanderley, Lurdes, Polonia, Victor. You all remained put even in those times where I was an enigma to you. Thank you for respecting my strangeness, my silence but for not giving up on me. You might not know this, but you gave some meaning to my life one way or another, and you made me feel like I 'belonged' to 'something'. You were and still are my Tribe, which kept me going when all felt lost and empty.

**To Marlene (aka) Tuxa:** Please continue to be the young wise, kind, and caring woman that you are. If only you knew how many times you filled my soul with your warm and God sent words. Thank you for your patience along the way. You were/are more than a friend, at times I felt like you were a mother talking to a daughter, and I needed that. I know some people do not take you seriously because of your funny character. But I do, and I respect you enormously. You are an inspiration and a true fighter, and everybody deserves a friend like you.

**To Tania:** Girl, the only good thing that came out of our relationship with our baby fathers is our friendship and our children. I am happy to have you and the girls in our lives. You also brought Rita and Raimonda to my life, and I feel blessed that I gain a sister and two bonus friends and nieces. I Love and care for you all very much. Thank you for your support and for loving my son, unconditionally. I will always have your back and support you in whatever I can.

**To my Primary teacher:** I hope that you are still alive and well. I hope to find you and to be able to thank you in person for the 'good' that you have done in my life. Your kindness remains with me to this day and gave me light in one of the darkest moments of my life. You cared for me and for your students and for that you will forever be one of the Angels of my Life.

**To my Publisher and Illustrator:** I must start by saying thank you to my friend Donna for introducing me to her cousins Marcia and Sam. Marcia is my publisher and Sam, my illustrator. God works in mysterious ways, and this cross-world was no doubt one of his works. We met years ago and who would have thought that we would end up working together on a project that is so close to my heart. Thank you, Marcia and all your team, for your guidance and teaching in this journey. Thank you for having me on your team and for believing in me. You are an inspiration, and I very much look up to you. Sam, thank you for listening to my demands and bring to light my ideas. You are very talented, and I always admired your work, so I feel extremely blessed to have this collaboration with you.

**To Stennett:** To the man that taught me how to love without pressures, to accept love without guilt, that allowed me to be myself and still respected me, cherished me, loved me and encouraged me to pursue my dreams and always remain true to myself and to others. You are a 'whole' man, a special one... a keeper. I feel blessed to have met you and to have you in my life. Thank you for always checking up on me and giving me strength when I doubt myself. Sometimes I wish I could see myself through your eyes because all I feel from you is love and admiration. I will always love you.

**To Jannette:** My adopted momma, it's beautifully weird how we connected without knowing each other. After reading your book, I understood why, I 'See' you as you 'See' me, and I am thankful that you accepted my invitation to write my Foreword. Thank you for listening to me and for supporting me on this journey. You are an inspiration to me and to many others. Keep doing great, I will be right behind you, following you and learning from your greatness.

**To Annette:** while writing this book, I realised how much patience you had with me. As my Manager, you did not have to put up to half of my tantrums, but you did, and you listened, and you 'saw' what others could not see. You protected me, and you gave me space to grow as an excellent and respectful professional. I am forever grateful for your kindness, my respect and admiration for you goes beyond words.

**To my first readers:** These are the people that read my manuscript first and encouraged me to pursue publication. I knew I wanted to publish it, but your words of support made me go an extra mile and exalt in myself my creative roots and mindset. This just to show that words have great power, so continue to use them wisely and kindly.

**To my friend that I 'lost' along the way:** I will forever be grateful for all the help you gave me with Gabriel. Without you, I would not be able to accept that job offer years ago. The same job that gave me financial stability and enabled me to keep the roof above my head and put the food on my table. Without your help, my son would probably be a damaged child as I could not be, for him, the mother he needed me to be. You gave me time and space to have time for myself and to look for help; no distance or strangeness between us will ever make me forget it. I wish you well, and I hope to tell you this to your face one day without resentment or hurtful feelings.

**To my Therapist, Ian:** You were the first person to tell me to write my life story. What seemed so crazy at the time, now is endeared and ready to come out of the oven. I will keep my promise and bring you a signed copy as soon as it is released. I have much respect for the work you and other professionals like you do. Keep doing great and helping and changing peoples' lives.

To you all, a massive thank you! You all impacted my life in one way or another. You all inspired or supported me in some way in my journey or during this book's writing, and I am very much appreciated for it. All I have for you is love because love is the base of all things that come from the Above. Stay grounded, stay truthful, stay humble and love beyond expectations or judgements.

# Foreword

When asked to write this foreword, I had no hesitation. Why? Aurea is me. I understood her the minute I saw her, and that was only a picture. Call it a sixth sense if you like, but intuition will do.

After several exchanges of messages, all I wanted to do was adopt her, I asked her if I could informally, and she accepted. After reading the manuscript of this book in its rawness, I knew immediately the answer to that initial 'why' why I saw myself in Aurea.

The adult addressing the child within and the need to seek answers. The buried questions never asked at all along with the scars not quite healed because they were concealed.

My dear dear Aurea 'I SEE YOU, and I appreciate you, you are no longer alone.

**Jannette Barrett Author of an Autobiographical Trilogy, They Never Saw Me, I Don't Know Who I am and Cries from their Cells**

# Chapter 1
## Wanuza – 'The truth behind the smile'

When I was six years old, my mother took me from Angola to Portugal on holiday. Before the end of the holiday, she started telling me it would be good for me to stay in Portugal because the schools were better, and it would be great for me. The problem was that in Angola, with the constant conflicts, sometimes schools would be closed for weeks and it wasn't safe at times. At the beginning I was happy to stay, as I knew the family I was going to stay with, and they were nice to us and always so welcoming. My mom made all the agreements with them: they arranged a price to be paid monthly for my staying, went to see a school for me, discussed the rules, and then she was off to Angola while I stayed behind. They were a family of five, but I only remember the name of the older daughter, Eva, her mom, Carla, and their neighbour, Judas.

Some things happen when you are a child, and your natural coping mechanism helps you forget, get numb over it or just pretend it never happened. That's exactly what happened to me. After I left the place where I was abused, I pretended my time there was just a bad dream and it was over now.

I have always been a resilient person. I am guessing that being sexually molested aged six teaches you to find ways to swirl through life and have hope of better days to come in order to be able to deal with the emptiness you constantly feel in your soul. In the beginning, you question if that is normal: is that the way adults love children? That's what he used to say to me: 'I love you Wanuza.' I questioned my mother's love – she had never done it to me, or any other relative of mine. I was confused, knew nothing, and no one explained anything to me; no one acknowledged me, no one 'saw' me but him. He saw me: a vulnerable, unloved and lost child. I was an easy target, obedient and quiet like a mouse. These people I lived with had no idea of the monster they had around their home. They were not nasty people, never mean, never laid a hand on, or shouted at me. Actually, they were humble and kind people, but also very busy, and very 'unaware' of me! As I was always so quiet, sometimes I wonder if they forgot I was still there?! I'm guessing I should be grateful, as it could have been worse.

I stayed with this family for a year, and during this time I grew close with Judas! As I mentioned, I wasn't 'invisible' to him. He would talk to me, ask about my day, teach me how to paint on canvas (because he was a canvas painter, an artist), and we would watch cartoons, eat together, and then we would play.

It was always the same play: he would ask me to get naked, lay me down on his bed and perform oral sex on me while I was playing with my naked Barbie doll. I didn't understand the playing, but I felt something, and it was a nice feeling of pleasure, so I guessed it was OK! He said I liked it and he told me that made him happy and gave him pleasure. I never touched him, and he never asked me to. Thankfully, he never tried penetration, and now I wonder if it was because I was too young or too small in my private areas (but I don't want to dwell on that thought a minute longer). However, he did try to introduce an object once (the handle of a brush) into my vagina; but as that hurt me, he stopped, and never tried again.

On that day he hurt me, I got scared. He'd never hurt me before; he was always so gentle and caring. I became frightened of being alone with him and started disliking him. All of a sudden it would annoy me to just look at him, but I was never rude, never unpleasant and never said NO! I was just like my Barbie doll: mute and always with a smile on my face. I had no voice, no emotions, no feelings, and I was always ready to play whenever he wanted to. After a while, I started hating playing with that doll. I remember finding the doll clothes, getting her dressed and putting her away somewhere and never touching her again. Until recently, I hated dolls: just looking at them in the shop would annoy me, and if I see a child playing with a naked doll, I always ask why she is naked, and I help the child get the doll dressed and give it back to them. But, just recently, I fully understood why: as I said, my defence mechanism made me forget that.

As days passed, I started to understand what he was doing to me was wrong, so I used to ask Mrs Carla to stay home, or to go outside to play with the other children from the neighbourhood until her oldest daughter, Eva, got back from school. Bear in mind that playing with those kids outside or in school wasn't my cup of tea either. They would bully me for the colour of my skin and my 'funny' hair. I was different to them, an object of curiosity; they would ask me random questions like if, in Angola, we lived in trees, ate bananas all day, or if we dressed in normal clothes.

I remember when Mrs Carla decided to cut my hair because they didn't know how to take care of it. No one asked me what I thought or explained to me what was going to happen; they just told me to sit down on the chair and shaved it all off. I sat down with a smile on my face and saw my hair going down to the floor. I bet you, they probably thought I was happy, as I didn't contest it, didn't cry, just accepted it and resigned myself to my insignificance. My feelings weren't important, and in fact I didn't even think I was allowed to have any (whatever feelings meant).

When I went to school on the Monday, all the other kids started throwing jokes at me. It was already difficult to be a black girl in a white environment, and with my hair chopped off it was even worse. My 'girlish' look was gone, and even I thought I looked like a monkey. My teacher, on the other hand, was nice and she looked just like me: black and with an unapologetic Afro! I remember she saw me sitting in a corner and she called me to a one-to-one! She said she would have a word with the other kids to stop picking on me, but she also needed me to understand something … So, she held my hands, looked straight into my eyes and said: 'Aurea, you are beautiful, your skin is beautiful, your hair is beautiful, you are loved, and you matter. Don't allow others to make you feel less than the beautiful girl that you are to me and to your mother, as I am sure she loves you very much. Believe in that and continue to smile because you have a lovely smile.'

I started to cry. I cried unconsolably and nonstop for a while! She tried to understand why I was crying so hard. Was it because of what your friends were saying? Was it something at home? Did I miss my mom? But after a while she just gave in, hugged me tight and just kept saying 'it's OK, everything is going to be OK, just let it go, it's OK'.

I sobbed and sobbed until I had no more tears to cry. I don't know what happened but, from the moment she held my hands and looked straight into my eyes, I swear I felt a divine power in me. Her hands gave me security and closeness, her eyes showed me kindness, compassion and love. Her words mattered and still matter, but her touch gave light to my soul: she gave me 'life'. I couldn't explain it to her as I didn't know how – all I knew was the transformation I was feeling inside. I now 'knew' people, the evil and the good, and could sense their energy: I wasn't 'naïve' anymore. I now had an intuition, was connected to my divine self. I believed in 'something' but didn't know what that 'something' was. But I knew about God: I heard about Him and went to His 'house' many times in Angola with my auntie Augusta and my cousin Patricia. I had forgotten about Him; but now I believed God sent my teacher as an angel to remind me of Him and all the good things He could do for us (me)! Again, I don't remember my teacher's name, but I will call her 'Angel' because, to me, she was one.

I started to spend more and more time outside with the neighbourhood children. I'd rather endure their bullying than have that man touch me again. I remember one afternoon he called me to come inside but I said 'NO' with a really upset face and a loud voice. I said: 'I am playing with my friends,' and by some miracle he just left and never tried again. They weren't my friends, they didn't even like me as a friend, but they would allow me to play with them as a child. For me, bullying was just part of it, and I was OK with that.

It's funny how your mind plays up. Most of these things I didn't remember any more (maybe that's why I can't remember my teacher's name). But, recently, more precisely in July 2019, I received a photo of myself aged six, and all the baggage I had been holding arrived with no check-in and tumbled me down big time.

5

The picture was sent by Eva, the daughter of Mrs Carla, and she meant well by sending it, but all she did was to open old wounds. I looked at the picture and felt out of breath and started crying, it was like seeing a ghost.

I was thrown back by that little child: so lost, unloved, lonely, afraid, mute – but always with a smile on her face! It all came up: the hurt, frustrations, rage, pain, everything I didn't know or didn't allow myself to feel during those times. It all came up: all the things I didn't say to that man, to my so-called friends, to that naïve and inattentive family 'taking care' of me, and to my mom for leaving me there with those strangers. I cried like a child – I wasn't thirty-seven years old anymore. I was her again. I was six, I was vulnerable, and I was feeling lost. I sat on my bed holding my knees to my chest, and I cried until I felt myself again. After that, I wept my tears, and I did what I learned in therapy: I closed my eyes and envisioned my old self talking with my younger self! I started by saying:

'Hello, beautiful girl. You have such a beautiful smile; I love your dimple!' I also held her hands, looked into her eyes and assured her she didn't have to smile all the time, that she was allowed to be sad and hurt and cry if something upset her. I told her that our life so far had loads of ups and downs, but we ended up OK, that right now we were happy, loved, had a 'voice', were in control of our life, that our smiles were genuine, that we had good and caring friends, a loving boyfriend and family, a happy home, a promising career on the horizon and a sweet, healthy, intelligent and gorgeous son.

'Beautiful girl, we made it. Thank you for teaching me resilience and to always hold on to 'something' or just for listening to the positive voices in your head. Thank you for never giving up; your strength brought us here.

Nevertheless, I apologise for leaving you behind all these years, for forgetting about you and ignoring all the times you tried to come out. You matter to me, you always mattered, and you will continue to matter. You are not alone; I am here with you and we are enough.'

Just like that, my younger self stopped smiling because she felt safe and happy she didn't need to put on a false smile anymore. We hugged and we cried. I cried until I fell asleep! That night I had a dream: we were on a beach I was plaiting her hair. (such beautiful curly hair, full of personality). We didn't say anything to each other; we were just there looking at the sunset while plaiting her hair, feeling peaceful and content. We understood each other now. There was no more 'she' or 'I' – from then on it was only 'we'. I now understand that all my life, the way I reacted to certain things in various situations, was based on the antagonised and oppressed child within myself. I now know better, and I owe it to 'us' to keep doing the work and always strive for excellence.

I woke up the next morning and, for the first time in my life, I felt whole! I felt complete – I'd found my missing piece of the puzzle. I said my morning prayers, got myself out of the bed, took my son to his activities and, instead of throwing myself into my normal mommy duties (cleaning and shopping), I decided to have a quality day with my son – everything else could wait. I was in the moment, feeling appreciative, with a big smile on my face because I could feel the divine in me!

**To Eva: Let's Break the cycle of silence'**

Eva: thank you for sending that picture. Without knowing it, you helped me heal. I believe things happen for a reason, that God creates bridges between what was and what needs to be. When you sent the picture, I felt so upset and unsettled, but now I appreciate you for that.

I did ask her about Judas. I don't even know if they are related or if he is just a family friend, as he used to live next door. I asked her if he was still alive. She said yes and asked me why. And I told her – just like that, I spilt the beans, without thinking, fear, or delay, no more secrets. We are free now, not victims, we can talk about everything without shame or guilt. Enough with the silence! I just vomited all my words out. So far, only my ex (Patrick), my therapist and Stennett (my boyfriend) know about that. I never told my mom, and my friend Dalila only knew because Patrick told her. No one else knows. I just felt that what's in the past should stay in the past. It didn't matter, and if I avoided the conversation, eventually it would disappear.

Eva did say she suspected and always wondered why I never said anything. That right there, upset me. My thought was: 'You suspected? And you never asked me anything? You never cared enough to investigate or bring it to your parents' attention? But you expected me to say something?! To say what you also didn't have the courage to say. You were a teenager, and you didn't feel powerful enough to say it out loud? How do you think I felt? WOW – that's messed up and unbelievable!'

Straight after, she said that guilt had consumed her over the years, and maybe that was why she was struggling to have children. She knew he did it to other girls and he also tried it with her niece, but they stopped it in time. But still he is a free man, because people around him adopted the silence code, which is common in cases like this, because they are afraid of 'what people will say' or do it, to 'protect the child'. She said her mom thinks the world of him and doesn't believe what people say about him. I told her he is a parasite, and one day I hope to have the opportunity to look into his face and tell him that. To tell him he didn't break my spirit with his evilness. What he did to me doesn't define me, but it does define his low, miserable self. Nevertheless, I would also say to him: I do forgive you. Not that you deserve any forgiveness, but I need peace of mind and to move on. I need to be able to say that to his face one day, and it will be the cherry on top of the cake.

I also said to Eva: 'Listen, I forgive you, and you also need to forgive yourself. We were both young, didn't know better – let's now choose to always speak up and not turn a blind eye to what needs to be addressed. Please trust that God has a plan for everyone and, in the right moment, you will be a mother.'

Just like that, I let them go. I dealt with what I had to deal with regarding that chapter of my life. I still want to confront Judas but, for now, I let him go. He is not important, he has no more power over me, my younger self, US! Therefore, we are FREE to move on and be HAPPY.

*'Now, every time I witness a strong person, I want to know: What darkness did you conquer in your story? Mountains do not rise without earthquakes.' – Katherine MacKenett*

# Chapter 2
# Family – 'The place where I feel more isolated'

My relationship with my family was always estranged: I always felt like I was a foreign, no one understood me, that I was constantly being judged and attacked for being 'quiet and private' with my thoughts.

My worst interaction was always with my mother. I can honestly say our relationship was one of love and hate. Once she told me she felt that, in another life, we probably slept with the same man (laugh).

I don't remember much of my interaction with my mom before she left me in Portugal. Some memories are blurred, others I just forgot. But I do remember my most painful and resentful parts with her. My mother was a single mother until I was five/six years old. It was just me and her. She worked in a great company in Angola as an account chief of department. She was good at her job, she was/is a hard-working woman, is passionate in everything she puts her mind to and is a woman of many talents. She was/is admired by many people for her perseverance, strength, ambition, kindness and compassion.

We used to live in a shared house with my auntie and her four children. The house only had two rooms; me and my mom would stay in one room and my auntie and her children in the other room. The house was in a social neighbourhood and everyone there loved and respected my mother. To this day when she goes there, people still call her 'Auntie Flora.' We often joke that my mother has nephews older than her, as no matter how old the person was, they would call her 'auntie.' I'm not trying to put her on a pedestal, but I think for many she was like Madre Teresa of Calcutta! It didn't really matter if she knew the person or not – if they were in need, she would just drop everything and go help them. I remember sometimes at work, some of her suppliers would offer her those big bags of rice, dry beans, pallets of drinks, milk, toys or clothes; my mother used to divide it in equal shares and give to the most needy families in the neighbourhood. She would make sure we had our share and also the rest of our extended family, but never forgot those in worse position than us.

I remember one night a girl in her twenties knocked on the door with an old lady with her and saying her grandmother was in a lot of pain. The poor woman couldn't talk; she was moaning in pain. My mother asked the girl to go wake up the neighbour that had a car and was as kind as she was (I don't remember his name). She laid the woman down on our sofa and started talking to her in an Angolan dialect (umbundu), maybe to calm her down or to understand what was going on. When our neighbour came, my mom told me to go to bed, and they rushed the old woman to the car and went to the hospital. That night, I wondered if my mom was also a doctor. There was nothing she could not do!

My mother, I came to understand, is an entrepreneur; a woman with a business mind that could have gone far in life and have tremendous success if she'd had the right opportunities and a good support system. That's how I

11

remember my mother: a superhero, capable of doing everything and always helping others.

For a long time, it was just me and her. When she was working, she would leave me with auntie Esmeralda, who was a family friend and like my second mother. On the weekends we would meet my mother's friends and go to the beach or just gather at their houses. Most of the time, I was the only child there, but I was happy to just be there with my mom and her friends. Life then was not perfect, but I remember being happy. I loved and admired my mother. She was also a fashion icon – always well dressed and the most beautiful woman I knew. I remember thinking many times: when I grow up, I want to be just like my mother!

Everything changed after she left me in Portugal. When she came back she was still my mother, but she was a stranger. She only left me for a year, and I was happy to see her again after that time, but I also felt the difference in me; she didn't have that amazing 'sparkle' I used to see in her (I just couldn't explain or understand, but I guess I was just upset to be left behind).

On top of that, she was pregnant. I remember feeling so betrayed: she left me there with those people and went to be happy with my stepfather and have babies. I felt a jealousy, rage and panic that she would leave me with these people for the rest of my life. But, again, I didn't cry. I didn't react – I just accepted and smiled the entire time, like I was happy with the news. I WASN'T! I hoped that wasn't her plan.

She came to pick me up to go back to Angola but, before that, we went to Brazil on holiday to meet my stepfather, as he was already there. My mother never asked me how it was living with those people! I know she didn't like the fact they cut my hair without asking her, and she was surprised
12

to find me a few pounds heavier. But, apart from that, she never asked, and she never knew what that man did to me, because I never told her. My teacher (Angel) did try to tell her something, or at least warn her. She set up a meeting with my mom, and instead of doing it in school, she asked my mom to go to her house. My mother was curious to know what she had to say, but instead of just me and her going, she took Carla and Eva with us. I saw the disappointment in my teacher's face when she opened the door. For one hour, my teacher went around subjects and ended up not saying whatever she wanted to say to my mother. But my mother noticed and commented to a friend: 'I think Wanuza's teacher had something important to tell me but didn't want to say it in front of Carla.' However, she never cared enough to go back and ask her.

Brazil was amazing. I actually ended up bonding with my stepfather. He was a man of few words, calmer and more relaxed than my mother, and more patient and funnier. We had a great, proper family holiday, just the three of us. It wasn't just me and my mother anymore: now I had a dad.

I never met my father. He never cared enough to come look for me. All I knew about him was that he had loads of women and children. My mother saved a picture of him but it's a bit blurred, so I was never able to see his face. If he passed me in the street, I wouldn't be able to recognise the man. All I know about him is his name: Carlos Alberto Silva Reis. However, my mother wasn't sure of that, as she told me she found a box with different IDs, with his face and different names. The man didn't even bother to register me when I was born, apparently: she had to ask a friend to go in his place and sign the papers in his place so I could have his name.

I also know she endured domestic violence from him. She never told me that, but I heard it from uncle Luis (her brother) years later. My uncle hated his guts. The main reason my mother left him was because she found out he was married! He had a wife in Luanda and was living with my mother in Huambo. She left him while pregnant with me at the age of nineteen. He made it pretty clear that, if she didn't want him, he had no obligation to me.

My mother told me once she was so happy she had a baby girl. She was so scared that, if I was a boy, she would hate me as much as she hated him. However, this is the same woman that would have constant arguments with me because I didn't want to go meet the man everyone said was my 'father'. Any other woman in her situation would be happy with their child's decision. Not my mother. She was always taunted by the idea I could end up getting married to a brother or relative of mine from my father's side (this was common in Angola in my times). She used to say: 'Wanuza, don't allow my story with your father to be your story with him! Someone needs to give the first step, and maybe this person is you.' How could she say that to me? What kind of mother encourages her daughter to go visit a so-called father that never cared enough to show his face. That used to make me feel so mad and upset with her!

I remember the first time I ever dreamed about him. I was seated in a white and bright place, and he came out of nowhere, dressed in white, and said: 'I am your father.'

To which I responded: 'So what? Leave me alone!'

He replied: 'I am sorry I wasn't there for you.'

And I said was: 'I will never forgive you. Leave me alone!'

14

I woke up the next morning with my heart feeling heavy. After a few hours, my mother called me to her room and told me a friend of hers reached out to say Carlos had died! I started to cry, not because I was sad, but because I felt relieved I didn't have to address that chapter ever again in my life. In my mind, that was done and dusted; I didn't have to argue with her again over him. I told her about my dream and she got upset that I didn't forgive him. She urged me to say a prayer that night and tell his spirit that, although I wasn't ready to forgive him, I honestly wished him to rest in peace. And I did what she told me – the last thing I need is his ghost taunting me for the rest of my life in my dreams.

After we got to Luanda (Angola), things were pretty much normal, just like any other family. Both my parents worked. I was in school, and weekends we would spend together at home, at the beach or visiting friends and family. Although I always called my Dad by his first name.

I liked him. At the beginning, not so much, as I was scared of men. I was scared he might do the same to me as Judas used to. So, when he would try to get close to me, I would be rude, distant or just ignore him. But, with time, he grew on me to the point where my mom would actually feel jealous of our relationship.

However, after my sister Vanessa arrived, everything changed. On 2nd February 1990, I woke up to find my mother seated on the floor of her room, breathing heavily and her forehead covered in sweat. I didn't know she was in labour, but as we were on our own at home, I asked her if she needed help, and she shouted at me to get out of the room and call the neighbour. In the meantime, my Dad came home with my auntie. My auntie took me to her home and my parents rushed to the hospital. Everything was so frantic that I was confused as to what was going on. Apparently, my mother went home the next day, but I was only able to see her and the baby after ten days, because on the same day my sister was born, I got chickenpox.

By the time I was able to go home, the dynamic of the family had changed – once again, I was invisible. My Dad only had eyes for his daughter, and my mother would only acknowledge me to shout at me because I did something that annoyed her, or to ask me to do something for her or the baby. I would often sit on my own to have dinner because they were having dinner together in the room while playing with the baby. At the same time, my mother started passing loads of responsibility to me, because she needed help around the house. After school, I always had to rush home – if I stayed behind playing with my friends, my mother would hoop my ass off. I had to help with the cleaning and the cooking – at the age of eight I knew how to cook rice, make any type of soup, stews and fry eggs. I wasn't allowed much around the baby, but I had to watch her while my mother took a shower every afternoon. It was a strange thing looking at that small creature, almost like looking at an extra-terrestrial. I had seen babies before, but never so close, so beautiful, innocent, fragile and dependent.

My Dad was over the moon. It was like he was learning to be a parent again, which was strange to me, because he had older children. One of them was Rui, who used to stay with us sometimes. I remember my mom trying to include him in everything and try to communicate with him, but he was just as quiet as me. We didn't have much interaction either, as he was way older than me.

Growing up around my sister was the most annoying thing I can remember. She was so spoiled, lacking humility, greedy, a show-off, self-centred, dramatic and so entitled. The list goes on and on! I used to hate playing with her because we were so different. She liked to play with dolls, I wanted to play with cars and colouring books, watch TV or just be quiet in one place. Vanessa was never quiet: she was used to being the centre of attention, and therefore she was too loud and an in-your-face personality. Also, she would mess all the toys around just because she could, and my mother would smack me when she didn't tidy them up. One time I had had enough and asked why I had to do it, and her response was: 'Because you are the oldest and you need to set the example!' My sister would do whatever, but if I was present, it was my fault because I saw it and didn't correct her. Everything she did or did not do was my fault, and the excuse was always the same: because you are the oldest and you need to set the example.

Gosh, I hated my sister, and I was starting to hate my mother too. I was the stepdaughter, not just to my Dad, but to my mother as well. I remember him saying a couple of times to my mom 'leave the kid alone' or 'don't hit the girl', and her response was always the same: 'She is my daughter. Don't tell me what to do!' So, he stopped interfering when my mother would shout, hit me, or just scold me for something I did or did NOT do. Sometimes I felt, because she couldn't smack or hit my sister, she would take it out on me. She could do whatever with me, but she wasn't allowed with Vanessa, as her Dad was very specific: 'Don't you ever lay down a hand at my daughter.' Until she was older, she never did.

They were both equally guilty for Vanessa's melodramatic and annoying behaviour. My Dad would give her whatever she wanted. If we went to the shop and she wanted something, she would put it in the shopping trolley without asking and he would pay for it. If my mother was around, she would try to contest it, but it was two against one! Plus, many times I heard my Dad say: 'It's my money – I do whatever I want with it!'

My mother wasn't working at the time so, after a while, I noticed she stopped fighting against them and just let them be. I saw my mother go from that independent woman ready to rule the world, to a dependent woman where her voice was getting cut off more and more every day. Her shine was gone. As before, she was used to doing her own thing, helping others and being a go-getter. But she was stuck in the house with two children, cleaning, cooking and worrying where her partner was late into the night, instead of being home with us. There was no structure in that house, but clearly there was a division: my Dad and my sister, my mother and me. My Dad's attention would be all for Vanessa; my mother's attention was in fighting for my Dad's attention against her little daughter. And me? Well, I was just a spectator of the show, but also the punchbag of my mom because all her frustrations would be thrown at me. Some women are cut out to be housewives, but my mother is not one of them, and that life almost drove her crazy. The constant arguments between them, the crying, jealousy, the making up. Then, start all over again!

It was scary and sad, and I always wondered, if he left her, would she still want me? It seemed the only thing holding our family together was that, even though she was always on his case, he was still willing to stay and come home every day. It seemed like he was her oxygen. Without him, would she function? Would she be capable of still being a mother? Would she be able to love me? The same way she used to be happy to see him come home, so was I. He always said, if he ever left, he would take Vanessa with him. But what about me? Would she want me, or would she leave me to go try and have them back on her own? Maybe I was the reason they fought so much? Maybe that's why she was so mean to me sometimes? Maybe they are not happier because I am in the way? I always wondered but, in those moments, I used to just go to my bed, close my eyes and pray for my Dad to come home.

## Do you hate me that much?

In 1992, there was a year of elections in Angola, and political tensions started all over the country. My parents decided it was best for us to go to Portugal and stay there for a while. We all went, including Rui. My Dad's parents lived in Olhao, Algarve (Portugal), and that's where we headed. His father's name was Augusto and his mother's Fatima. Me and my mother were so happy we were going to meet them. My grandmother from my mother's side died when I was five, so I was excited to have new grandparents (I don't even remember why). And I am guessing my mother was happy, for the first time in her life, to have a relationship where she had contact with the other half of the family.

But the reality was completely different, as my Dad failed to tell us his parents were very white, and although they lived in Angola for many years, they did not like black people (especially in their house). My Dad was happy to introduce them to us, as his parents were old and with a few health problems, so, he wanted us including my mother to stay there and look after them. From the first day, we felt the animosity coming from them. They looked down on me and my mother, but they were nice to Rui and Vanessa. It came to light that, although Rui was darker than me, he was also their blood and so was Vanessa. Me? I was a bastard, and my mother wasn't married to their son so, in their own words, she was just his concubine. I remember one of Fatima's friends came over and, while in the living room, the friend said: 'Your daughter-in-law is very beautiful and very nice!'

Fatima replied: 'She is not my daughter-in-law as she is not married to my son. As far as I am concerned, she is just his concubine!'

I didn't even know what that meant, so I asked my mother. She cried a few tears instead of explaining to me what it meant. On another occasion, my Dad's sister (Clara) came to visit and, as soon as she was introduced to me, I started calling her auntie. Where I come from, and the way I was raised, it's just a polite way of showing respect for your elders. In fact, I used to also call Fatima and Augusto nana and papa. I came to find out that they hated me treating them or calling them in that way. One time, very abruptly, she told me I wasn't her granddaughter, and then told Clara to not allow me to call her auntie either. Clara's response was: 'She is just a child and there is no harm in it.'

Her response was: 'I don't want to be associated with these people.'

This was my introduction to my Dad's parents! I always liked the rest of his family; I just wasn't very keen on his parents. My parents bought a house in Olhao and we all moved in, including Fatima and Augusto. After that, my Dad soon left for Angola, and my mother stayed with us until Christmas. She arranged schools for me and Rui and, after Christmas, she informed us both that we needed to take care of each other and help his grandparents around the house, as she was heading back to Angola with my sister Vanessa to be with our Dad.

I felt like laughing when she said that. I remember thinking: 'These people have shown their dislike for our presence in their life and you want me to stay here with them? WOW, you must really hate me!'

But I didn't do anything. Again, I just accepted my fate and resumed myself to my insignificance. After all, there was nothing I could do. The day she left; I cried all night. Rui heard me crying and came to my room to comfort me; he brought me some comic books and read some stories to me. He was funny and silly. I have come to understand now that was his coping and defence mechanism. He was always joking about something or trying to make people laugh about everything and nothing. Me and him grew closer together, to the point where I started having feelings for him! He knew and kept his distance, first because he was older than me and, second, because 'technically' we were brother and sister.

I remember one day he fell asleep on the sofa and I went to cover him with a blanket and then kissed him on the lips. He woke up, looked at me, startled, pushed me out of the way and went to his room. I never felt so embarrassed in my entire life and was scared he would tell his grandparents or our parents. Thank God he never did but, after that, he kept even more distance between us. If we were home alone, he would just stay in his room, or out with his friends. I felt alone again, with no one to talk to.

At school things were hard. I was the only black girl in school; therefore, I was a monkey AGAIN! I stayed in that school for two years, and during those years I do not have one happy memory at all. My years being bullied in the primary school in Cacem (Lisbon) were bad, but here it was a different level. Children can be so mean. Every day, someone would call me negro or monkey or whatever they could think of. They would also slap me really hard in my back, or make me fall in front of everyone, so they could have a public laugh. Once, a girl came to me with scissors, cut off a piece of my hair and started running around showing it to everyone, then told me she was going to give it to her mother to wash the pans with at home. Another time, a guy emptied a bin over my head; the cleaning lady saw it and told me I needed to clean the mess up, as if I had started or provoked the situation. I remember kneeling and picking up the rubbish while everyone around me was laughing and making jokes. If that wasn't enough, someone else threw a banana at me and said: 'You forgot this!' I felt deeply humiliated and broken, and once again I hated my mother for leaving me behind.

However, I didn't let them see my tears. I stood tall in front of them, but I let myself go when I got to my room in the afternoon. I started having suicidal thoughts. Wouldn't it just be easier if I died? I could take rat poison before bedtime: if it killed rats, it would kill me too. I was sure my mother would be happy with that – it would be one less problem for her. I lay down and I dwelled on that thought for ages: what did I have to lose? No one would miss me. In a very robotic way, I went to our shed, picked up the rat poison, mixed it with a soup spoon in a glass of water and took it to my room to drink before bedtime.

I held that glass with all the strength (as I was shaking at same time) I had in my hands, and I cried. I cried my sadness, my weakness, my blackness, my hair, my pain, my mental exhaustion and my loneliness away. I cried until a voice in my head told me: 'Not today – put that glass away!'

And so, I did. I went to the toilet, threw it away and went to bed. That night, I dreamed I was running freely and happily in a camp of sunflowers. It was MAGICAL! I can still hear myself giggling, dancing and jumping around; I can still feel it like it was REAL!

## Still I Rise
*By Maya Angelou*

*You may write me down in history*
*With your bitter, twisted lies,*
*You may tread me in the very dirt*
*But still, like dust, I'll rise.*

*Does my sassiness upset you?*
*Why are you beset with gloom?*
*'Cause I walk like I've got oil wells*
*Pumping in my living room.*

*Just like moons and like suns,*
*With the certainty of tides,*
*Just like hopes springing high,*
*Still I'll rise.*

*Did you want to see me broken?*
*Bowed head and lowered eyes?*
*Shoulders falling down like teardrops.*
*Weakened by my soulful cries.*

*Does my haughtiness offend you?*
*Don't you take it awful hard*
*'Cause I laugh like I've got gold mines*
*Diggin' in my own back yard.*

*You may shoot me with your words,*
*You may cut me with your eyes,*
*You may kill me with your hatefulness,*
*But still, like air, I'll rise.*

*Does my sexiness upset you?*
*Does it come as a surprise*
*That I dance like I've got diamonds*
*At the meeting of my thighs?*

*Out of the huts of history's shame*
*I rise*
*Up from a past that's rooted in pain*
*I rise*
*I'm a black ocean, leaping and wide,*
*Welling and swelling I bear in the tide.*
*Leaving behind nights of terror and fear*
*I rise*
*Into a daybreak that's wondrously clear*
*I rise*
*Bringing the gifts that my ancestors gave,*
*I am the dream and the hope of the slave.*
*I rise*
*I rise*
*I rise.*

After that, I wasn't the same. The next day when I woke up, I felt different, powerful. My weakness was gone, and I was ready for a fight. I remember this girl came in my direction as soon as I got to school, and I looked her straight in her face and said: 'You touch me, and I will punch you in the face!'

I still lost the fight, as she and her friends all jumped on me. But I fought – and I fought the day after that, and the next one, until they got tired of picking on me. It wasn't about winning or losing, but about standing up for myself, as no one else would. Eventually, I made some friends: they would feel sorry for the stupidity and ignorance of their own, kind but couldn't really do much. I remember my colleague, Milene, saying to me once: 'Why don't you just ignore them, I think it will be better!'

And I said: 'I ignored, and I was silent for too long. No one can shut me up now! From now on, I will fight!' Until two years ago, that was the attitude I carried around with me: reacting without thinking, fighting for everything that didn't sit well with me, having an attitude or creating conflicts in situations where I could have just easily walked away. An angry little girl still trying to defend and stand up for herself against the world.

## 'All seems well when you have a tribe'

My mom eventually decided to move me out of that house. My parents would be back and forward between Angola and Portugal, staying with us for the Christmas and summer holidays. In the summer of 1994, my mother arrived alone and distressed in Olhao. She said Vanessa was with her auntie and that we needed to pack our things and go. She was four months pregnant (if I remember correctly) and arrived on a Friday night before we left on Saturday afternoon. It was like we were running from the police or something. She gave no explanation, to me or to anyone else; all she said was we were going to Lisbon, to her auntie's house. We put all we needed in the car and left.

During the two-and-a-half-hour drive, my mother cried most of the way. I knew not to ask questions when my mother was in that state. But, as I sat there, I felt sorry for her. I didn't know what was going on or what happened, but her crying was worrying and heart-breaking. To make matters worse, she lost the baby due to all the stress she was under. I remember, after a few days in her auntie Joana's home, I turned and said to her: 'Mom, what happened with your belly? It's getting smaller instead of bigger.'

When I said that, both her and her auntie started talking in an Angolan dialect, went to the bedroom and closed the door. All of a sudden, they came out of the room, called a taxi and rushed to the hospital. When they came back home, my mother was silent, so her auntie just said the baby died and to leave her alone as she needed to rest. My mother told me years later that the baby was dead inside of her for two days, but she was so cut up by her drama and stress with my Dad and his family that she didn't realise the baby hadn't moved at all, until I made the remark about her belly.

Living with my mother's auntie was all right. I called her 'grandmother'. She would always be favourable toward her real grandchildren but that, for me, was minimal. Moving to Vale da Amoreira with my mom's family was the best thing my mother had done so far for me. Her auntie wasn't perfect, but compared with everything else I had endured, she was pretty perfect to me. Vale da Amoreira is known to be a place with many ethnic neighbourhoods, and the predominant background is black people from Cape Verde, Guinea Bissau, San Tome and Angola. I was home and away, and in school I finally had a tribe. There I made good friends, and a few of them are still my friends today. There I found my ground; school was easier and fun, and every day was almost a joyful day. I liked it there.

My best friends were Vania, Vanda and Samira. I was always with them, especially Vania and Vanda; together we were the three Vs. We were always in each other's houses or outside of our homes just talking and making jokes, talking about everything and nothing. Everybody knew us. Some people liked us, and others didn't, but we were cool with that. My mother seemed to also be happy to see me with good friends, and she made sure she met my friends' parents when she was around in the holidays.

Vania lived with her grandmother, a sweet old lady that became our grandmother too, and Vanda lived with her mother and her older brother. They became my family; we cared for each other. With time my mother started feeling jealous of my relationship with my friends. She would say that I cared more about my friends than my family.

In fact, I did! All my life I lived 'alone': the people around me changed, but I was alone. There was never a unified front, in our family or between me and her. But now that I was grown and making friends, she wanted me to stop everything when she was around for me to go and do things with her. I wasn't keen on it. Apart from being my mother, there was nothing else that united us. When she got pregnant with my sister Jasmine, I did get close to her. I heard her saying to her auntie that my Dad didn't want the baby, and for some reason that made me sad for her, but more for the baby. I remember going to bed at night and thinking: 'Don't worry baby, I will love you. I want you here and you will be loved!'

So, I glued myself to my mother. I would help her with everything, go with her everywhere, and for the first time we started bonding. We even found things we liked in common: books and plants. We would talk about everything, and for the first time I would ask things about her and her past and she would respond without shouting or shutting me off. At the age of fifteen, I was getting to know my mother for the first time.

When Jasmine born, I was so happy and so in love with that little white baby. My first love was Jasmine; it was like she was my daughter. At the time I couldn't explain the feeling, but now that I have a son I understand. I used to do everything for her, apart from bath and feed her, as my mother was breastfeeding; but if I could have done that too, I would! Vanessa, on the other hand, was so jealous and would do everything for attention. I felt like my job was to protect Jasmine from Vanessa, as I was afraid she would do something mean to the baby: my baby.

Eventually, my mother got back to Angola with Jasmine and Vanessa. The day she left, I felt like someone took my heart away. I couldn't breathe. She was taking my baby away from me, but there was nothing I could do because the baby wasn't mine. That day, I fell out of love again with my mother. I thought what she did was cruel: she gave me hope of better days between us, she gave me Jasmine, and then she took it all away without considering my feelings or without a warning. I thought that after that we had Jasmine, she would stay in Portugal for good.

It took me a minute to get over that, but having Vania and Vanda around helped. I never told them my inner struggles, and I know that sometimes they failed to understand my dark behaviours, my quietude, my relationship with my family and my difficult personality. I was always upset, always complaining about my family, sometimes maybe sounding ungrateful and mean. Other times, if we were having fun, I would want that moment to last indefinitely, and all they wanted to do was go home or go mind their own business. I was also more childish than them; they were quite mature for fifteen years old, but I wasn't. I was very responsible but immature, and naïve on so many levels. But still they were patient with me, and with them, I learned a lot. I was a ticking time bomb ready to explode every five minutes if someone told me the wrong thing or looked at me in the wrong way. But my friends kept me grounded and taught me to chill and have a laugh.

My parents bought a house in Vale da Amoreira and, after a few years of going back and forward, my mother decided to settle in Portugal. By then we were even more estranged, so the fact she was moving for good left me in panic. I didn't know how to live with her/them anymore. They were a family, but I didn't feel like I was part of it. It was always so strange seeing them coming during the holidays together, having their private jokes, talking about the things they used to do in Angola and family and friends' gatherings. And I would just sit there, feeling like an outsider. We used to have a good time in the holidays: my Dad loves to travel, so we would always go somewhere and have a good family time, but they had a family dynamic and I didn't feel like I fitted in.

To make matters worse, in Angola my parents had a housekeeper, so both my sisters wouldn't do anything at home. Coming to Portugal, it was the same old story of the 'older' sister. They would do nothing, so I had to do everything. If I talked back, it would be a problem. They would talk back to my mom in ways that I never dared, but if it was me, things would escalate to the point where she would stop talking to me for days and treat me like I wasn't welcome in her house. I would avoid spending any time at home, and the fact that at the time I was working and studying made life a bit easier.

## The worst is still to come

I often hear that through difficult situations people tend to come together. I agree with that. One Easter (around 2003/04), my mother told us that our uncle from Switzerland was coming to spend Easter with us and she expected everyone to be present at the table, as he had some news to tell us. This was all very good, as we loved him, and he was always welcomed, but the way she said it left us curious. I wondered if he was going to get married again. On the day I brought my boyfriend home with me and my mother got annoyed with that and told me it was supposed to be just family. I thought to myself, 'What's wrong with this woman? She's known Carlos for one year now; what's wrong with him having lunch with us?'

During lunch there were awkward silences, and my mother was strangely quiet. When we finished lunch and after we cleaned the kitchen, my mother politely asked my boyfriend to go home as we needed to have a family meeting. I was livid with her, 'What was so important that he couldn't hear or at least wait in the other room?' My uncle calmed me down and began by saying: 'What I am going to tell you is going to be hard on you guys, but it has been even harder on your mother. So, I urge you to find compassion in your hearts to not discriminate her or alienate her. She is already suffering enough, and she needs all the support that she can get, especially from you guys! You know about your Dad's indiscretions over the years? Unfortunately, he wasn't just being indiscreet, he was also not being careful; and thanks to that he caught HIV and passed it on to your mother. Apparently, she's had it for a while and only found out because she had a miscarriage and during the examinations the doctor told her. She has confronted your father and he did say that he'd known he had it for a while now but failed to inform her. She doesn't want anyone else knowing as people are still very judgmental and ignorant regarding HIV; but we both think it is important that you know. We excluded Jasmine from the conversation because she is too young, but at the right time she will know.'

My world collapsed. The room was spinning. 'I can't breathe, I can't breathe. I am going to throw up. I can't breathe.' I looked around and my sister Vanessa bolted out of the door. Jasmine was outside with my uncle's girlfriend. My uncle was holding my mother's hand, and my mother was just sitting there with her head down, crying inconsolably. I could see shame written all over her face. No, no, no! This is not your fault, mom (I thought). So, I got out of my seat and gave her a hug and cleaned her tears. I had nothing to say, but I wished I did as I could feel her pain, her shame, her sadness and her fear of rejection.

After she calmed down, I went to see my boyfriend (today, I wish I had never left). I was so distressed that I couldn't hide from him what happened. I know it was a shock for him too, but I was expecting a bit more compassion from his side. However, he made the situation about himself, saying that we needed to get tested, that he was always very scared of these things, asking me what I was going to do and when we should make an appointment. He never asked me how I was or, even more importantly how my mother was? But that was Carlos: very self-centred, very intelligent, but also very ignorant when it came to certain aspects of life. I forgave him for that thought – that wasn't his business to deal with – but a bit of compassion and support would have been nice.

I came home late that day and Vanessa was nowhere to be seen, or the morning after. I know me and her always had an estranged relationship, but I knew what she was feeling or thinking (you know your family). She was so close to her father in her childhood; no one could say anything about him, to her he was perfect. But for a few years all she'd had from him were disappointments. The first one was when she found conversations between him and his mistress on our home computer. She called my mother and showed her all she found. Her father then had the guts to say to my mother that he never expected my sister to betray him like that (laugh). He even stopped talking to her and began being distant with her. Vanessa didn't care: one thing me and my sisters all have in common is that we can't stand betrayal. He didn't just cheat on my mother: he betrayed all of us, and especially my sister Vanessa's trust, as she used to believe in him 100 per cent and defended him like a lion. I guess that for her this was the final cut, the one that hurt the most and took away the last hope of reconciliation between them. But right then I needed her to deal with her feelings in a grown-up manner. I needed her to be there for my mother: our mom needed us, and Vanessa disappearing was 'punishing' my mom and not my Dad. Eventually, she came home, and things were 'normal', or at least we tried to act like that. My uncle left after two days and we never addressed the issue again until years later. Until this date, my Dad never had the guts to sit with us and address the issue or apologise to my mother for what he did to her. Nothing!

He visited in the summer of that year and I was expecting a family meeting with both … Nothing! No ownership, no remorse, no guilt. Nothing at all. Life continued like NOTHING had ever happened. They dropped that bomb on us, asked for us to keep it secret and expected us to just accept it, like it is something that happens to everyone and we should be OK with it.

I completely lost respect for both. I thought my mother was a victim of my Dad's monstrosity and, as such, she should 'act', do something about it, such as take him to court, separate from him. I DON'T KNOW. But do *something*. And, as for him… Who does that? Who finds out that he has a sexually transmitted disease and says nothing to his partner? WHO? How does he live with himself? HOW?

32

As years passed, my relationship with them deteriorated. My mother was always trying to change me with her personality. Everything she said to me was always: 'If that was me ... in your place I would do ... if I was your age...'! Well, I didn't want to be her, and the more she would try to control me, the more I would withdraw. I convinced myself I was a tenant in that house. I didn't pay rent, so as such my payment was to clean and help where I could without causing any fuss. I stopped complaining about my sisters not participating in any of that, and I would stay away from home as much as possible. When at home, I would just stay in my room reading, sleeping, studying or just looking at the ceiling and dreaming of far way. That used to drive my mom crazy, and because she couldn't get to the core of me, she would just use everything to cause an argument, or as soon I was home, she would start shouting about something that has nothing to do with me but find a way of making it my fault.

I remember one time I came home around midnight. The kitchen was a mess. I said 'hi', went to the kitchen, grabbed a glass of water and said goodnight. She said: 'Before you go to bed, please clean the kitchen.' That day I was so tired; I'd worked all day, then had university at night. I wasn't having it, so I said: 'Your daughters were home all day doing nothing and now they are sitting in the living room still doing nothing. Why don't you ask them to clean the kitchen?' She replied: 'Because I am asking you and you are also my daughter'! I said: 'No, I am not doing it. I am sick of this.' She cut me off, saying: 'And I am sick of your attitude. You come and go from this house like you pay bills and we owe you something. It's clear that you don't like any of us and living with us is like a burden to you. For that reason, I want you to go. I will give you two months to find a place and move out, but until then you will clean that kitchen, or you can move out tonight.'

WOW. Words failed me. This woman had so much to say to me, to put me down, but she had done or said nothing to the man who destroyed her life. What did I do to her? I never brought any problems home: I never used drugs, I had a job, I was studying, I had good friends that she knew and approved of. I had a boyfriend that, although she wasn't keen on, she had no criticisms of. I helped around the house more than my sisters. What else did she want from me? It was so clear that I wasn't part of this family, that she would do everything to protect them and do anything to hurt my feelings and humiliate me. I felt rage, felt myself screaming inside. I wanted to slap everyone and run away from there. But I cleaned that kitchen and then I went to my room and I cried my rage away.

The next day, I was off work, so I woke up early and went to the beach (being close to the sea helps me think). I relived the night before again, and again, and again in my head – while getting ready to go, in the car and at the beach. I was numb. I couldn't comprehend the injustice, the constant arguments, the years of alienation, the division. Why did she hate me so much? I couldn't think any more, I was so tired, lost, EMPTY! As I sat there looking at the water, I felt it 'calling' me; the sound of the waves on the sand seemed like voices telling me to get inside and let go, just let it all go away. I don't know how to swim, so, I knew what to do. I was blank inside: it was like I was hypnotised by the sound of the water, as I was walked far into the water. It was like my body was dancing with the water – a silent melody, me and the water, the water pulling me and letting it go, my emptiness and my loneliness – I just wanted to go AWAY!

It was so quiet there. So peaceful. I felt like I was flying. A voice was shouting my name: 'WANUZA, WANUZA, WANUZAAAAA.' I recognised the voice but I didn't know exactly who it was, so I followed her.

A surfer took me out of the water. I was unconscious for a while. I guess he did CPR to bring me back. He asked me what happened, and I lied to him, said I had a cramp then panicked and started drowning. He asked me if I was all right or if I needed a lift somewhere or perhaps to call an ambulance. I said I was all right and I was driving; I just needed a few more minutes. After a while, I said thank you and left. As I sat in my car, I started crying and talking with God: 'That man did not know my name, so who was calling me? You keep saving me, you keep bringing me back … for what? What do you have in place for me, Lord? Please show me the way because I am tired of this life and this family of mine. I need a sign, just give me a sign.'

I went to meet my latest boyfriend Pedro in the afternoon and told him what happened (not at the beach) the night before. I asked him if he could help me look for a house. We spent the rest of the afternoon looking at some ads and visiting some landlords he knew. But after a week of no luck, he turned around to me and said: 'You know I have the house in Moita and I am looking for a tenant? Why don't we move in together? We've been seeing each other for a year or so, we both work, and I think we could give it a try. What do we have to lose?'

Exactly! What did we have to lose? More importantly, what did I have to lose? That same day, I went home and told my mother that, by the end of the month, I would move out.

## 'Addressing the wounds'

Skipping ahead to 27th of December, 2015, and I'd been with Pedro for 8 years. We lived together in Portugal for one and half years, but then decided to move to England. Me and Pedro had been separated for a year and taking care of our son Gabriel on my own while working full-time had proved challenging. My friend Dalila (who I met through Pedro's brother Miguel) helped me with him any time she could, but I tried to do most of it on my own, as he is my responsibility. My mother worried about us and called constantly to find out how we were. Eventually, she decided to pack her things up in Portugal and move to the UK to come and help me with my son.

After I moved out of the house and moved in with Pedro, things changed between me and mom. At the beginning, I was distant and didn't show up at all, but she would call and come around. Sometimes it was just to say hi, sometimes just to talk about my sisters and how they were doing her head in and didn't do anything or help around the house. Other times it was to talk about my Dad and their estranged relationship. At the beginning I found it funny and disrespectful; why did she want to be at my house and talk about her family? I didn't care. I'm out now, just leave me alone, I thought.

But then, the more I was growing into my relationship with Pedro and into an adult, I started to understand her and be more compassionate toward her. Plus, my mother didn't have friends in Portugal: she didn't go out, didn't work, so I realised she was lonely (I understood that feeling) and I became more of a friend, somewhere she could just go for few hours, or call and take out to share whatever was on her chest. It's funny how I used to give her advice like I was the mother, and she was the child (especially when it came to my dad).

When I moved to the UK, we became closer. She would call every Friday night just to make sure everything was all right. We became good friends, would tell each other everything. Our relationship was good, but not healthy, as the wounds were still there (deep down). We never addressed them, so they never healed. Unhealed wounds start bleeding or get infected.

Given that we were in a 'good' space, when she offered to come and live with me, I didn't see a problem. She had been separated from my father for three years, and I felt that perhaps she needed a change in scenario. I needed the help and Gabriel could grow up with a grandmother around. What could be wrong with that?

The problem was that, on top of the existing baggage between us, she was also bringing her own personal baggage with my dad. She was feeling stuck with her life and hurt to be left for another woman. In her own words, although she understood everything he had done to her, she still felt they should be together until death. She believed he owed her that. From what I recollect, she wanted me/us (daughters) to 'save' her: she would come to UK and her life would magically change. I had to live her problems and try to fix them. How could I fix her life if I was trying to fix my own?

That Christmas of 2015, my dear friend Elisabete came to spend the season with us. I was so excited that Beta as I call her was coming over (she is like a sister to me). Having her there, with my mother and my son, I was expecting this to be the best Christmas of all. We all needed that Christmas to be good and magical. Beta was upset that she couldn't go to Portugal to spend it with her family because of work. My mother was still reliving everything bad that had happened to her in the last years with my dad. And me and Gabriel just wanted a reason to celebrate and be happy, as my separation from Pedro was really hard on him. Living in a foreign country, it's always lovely to be surrounded by people you love and trust. I might have my issues with my mom – and she had never said that she loved me – but I knew deep down I could trust my life and my son's to her. To me that equalled love.

Elisabete, is my ride or die chick: the friend that has seen me cry more than anyone else, the one that tells it as it is, knows my demons, my flaws, my good side, my strength, my bad moods, my qualities, and most of my secrets. I say 'most' because I never told her before about my abuser (until recently). She wasn't ready to hear that, and I wasn't ready to tell her. Elisabete is a person that, when she loves you, she lives your pain, she protects you, she takes on your battles, and she fights for you. She's a true Scorpio that loves you or hates you. To know that part of my past would break her, and she would probably hate my mother more than I hated her at times. I didn't want that, or for her to see me as a victim, I wouldn't be able to stand that kind of feeling from her. But I knew that, eventually, I would tell her. But it had to come from a place of healing and hoping that she would take it as a piece of information with empathy, comprehension and love (and that's exactly what happened when I told her).

As I mentioned before, my mother always seemed to be jealous of the friends I had. It seemed to me like she was fighting for my attention. It was like trying to divide myself between my friend and my mother. The strike for me was when she told me that my sister was having a baby in March and she would like to go. I said, if that is the case, you should buy the ticket ASAP, so it doesn't get too expensive. Then she started going on and on about the fact that she was just one person, and she had to divide herself for all of us. I was confused; what was the problem? Vanessa was having a baby, you want to go help her, so go! She turned around and said: 'But you also need my help. I came here because you needed me; I am only here because of you and Gabriel.'

That right there pissed me off, so I said: 'No, no, no, NO! You are here because you wanted to come. You called me and you asked me if it was OK for you to come and stay here, and that you could be a good help for me with Gabriel. Now don't come and play the victim in front of my friend and make me look like an ungrateful child because that is not the case. And as much as I appreciate your help, good or bad, I was surviving on my own. And things like what you just said, that's the reason why I am always so reluctant to ask for help from anyone especially you. So, if you want to go, GO! But don't use me or my son as an excuse to not do whatever you want or need to do. Gabriel is my responsibility, and not yours.'

She didn't say anything else that night, but the following day she was unpleasant. Her energy was negative; she would be pleasant to my friend but give me the silent treatment. I chose to ignore it because I didn't want it to ruin my Christmas. I promised my friend a stress-free Christmas holidays and I was trying to save the best that I could from it.

That same night, me, Beta and Dalila were going to a Block Party in town (Wolverhampton). We started drinking and getting ready and, meanwhile, Gabriel started getting a temperature. So, I hesitated to go out and told my friends that I was feeling bad for leaving him. OMG, it was like I called my mother names. Out of nowhere she started shouting at me, saying that I thought she was incompetent, that it seemed like she'd never had kids and wasn't trustworthy to take care of my child.

At first, I was perplexed, looking at her and at my friends and thinking 'what the hell is going on? I know I'm drinking, but I'm not that drunk yet!' At the same time as she was talking, I felt this rage growing inside of me, boiling more and more until I exploded and started shouting at her: 'How dare you put words in my mouth! How dare you try to humiliate me and put me down in front of my friends? How dare you try to ruin my happy time with them? You did all of that while I was in YOUR house and I swallowed all of it because it was your house. Now you come to my HOUSE and you want to do the same? Make me feel shit in my OWN house, disrespect me in front of my son and my friends, treat me like that little child with no voice that would do everything to please you and still it was never enough, was never good enough. There is always a BUT with you, always a criticism, always a negative remark. I went to university because of you, to please you, to make you feel proud of me, but even that wasn't good enough. I paid for the ticket for you to come and watch my graduation and you managed to ruin my day with the same kind of attitude you are showing right now (because she wanted the attention on her, and I was trying to accommodate my friends at same time). What the hell is wrong with you? Can't you live in peace? What the hell do you want from me? To make me crazy? I am tired of you and our bullshit relationship. I am tired of doing things to please you. I have never been good enough for you and I never will, and you know what? I don't give a shit anymore. I don't care if you are my mother: you are not going to treat me like shit anymore, especially in my house and in front of my son. In this house, if you want respect, you better treat me with the same respect you expect from me. In this house I want love, I want peace, I want happiness. If you don't know how to live like that, then maybe it is time for you to go home.'

While I was shouting all this, and more things that I don't remember, Beta and Dalila tried to take me outside. Gabriel and Dalila's kids were afraid, and my mother was sitting on the sofa looking at me in shock. I was crying and shaking. They pulled me outside. I was only wearing a t-shirt, but I was so enraged that I couldn't feel the cold. All those years of disappointments, rage, anger, lack of empathy, lack of love – everything was coming out right there.

They didn't let me in the house again. We went to the club and I drank to forget. I am not much of a drinker, but that night alcohol felt like water. I cried, I laughed, I danced, and for a few hours I forgot everything. Beta took care of me, cleaned me, brought me home, cried with me and dried my tears up. She said something I will never forget that helped with my healing: 'It will be hard from now on, but it needed to be said, you needed that moment. The message was not delivered in the best manner, but I think it reached the destination exactly as it should. It's now up to the receiver to grab it and understand or not understand and work from there. You did your part, now rest and wait!' I remember saying to Beta: 'There is nothing to wait for, and if she is waiting for an apology, she can wait. I am not going to apologise. Everything I said, I felt it, and I mean it.'

My mother went back to Portugal two months later! Those months were horrific: we weren't talking to each other and Gabriel was in the middle of all of it. My house wasn't my house anymore. I gave her the power, and she took control of my home, my child and my sanity. I felt unwelcome in my own home, unloved and disrespected by my own mother and son (as Gabriel was now very attached to her and would only listen to her). Once again, I chose to ignore her. She wanted a fight, wanted me to throw her out so she could tell people what I did and how I treated her. I wasn't going to do that to my own mother. I'm not that person, never was and never will be.

At the time, I was starting to see a guy called Patrick, so I began spending more time at his house, and I would go home just to see my son once or twice a week. Eventually, she gave up and left! It all happened when Gabriel's dad came from Angola to visit him, so I said to her that he was going to pick him up. The next minute, I received a message from Pedro saying my mother left my house keys with him and said she was leaving for good. As horrible as it might sound, I felt relief. I felt happy. I was supposed to stay at Patrick's the whole weekend, but I chose to go home, clean and move things around. I lit some candles around the house, opened a bottle of wine and took a bubble bath. That night I said to myself: 'I will never talk to my mother again, until she acknowledges that respect has two ways, and that love and vulnerability are essential in any healthy relationship.'

*Pay attention to your patterns. The ways you learned to survive may not be the ways you want to continue to live. Heal and Shift.*

*Dr. Thema Bryant – Davis*

No one can live an entire life trying to please someone that is not happy with herself and keeps taking her frustration out on others. I prayed for her every day. I was determined to not talk to her, but I was sending love in her direction and straight to her heart, and I was asking God to guide her and give her some enlightenment and purpose in her life. I didn't give up on my mother (and I never will), but I needed space from her. I needed to break the cycle of arguing then brushing it all under the carpet and starting again like nothing ever happened. This time, if we were to talk again, things needed to be done properly, issues needed to be addressed, problems needed to be resolved. I wasn't going to entertain that kind of nonsense anymore.

She used to call my house to speak with Gabriel. I knew it was her, so I would just tell my son to answer the phone. They would speak for a while and I would switch off. It never bothered me: my fight was with her and had nothing to do with Gabriel and I wasn't going to be in the middle of their love for each other.

We remained estranged for almost two years! In the middle of 2017, I received a message from her, asking how I was, saying how much she missed me and how much she loved me and Gabriel. Clearly, something was changing, as I had never heard her using the words 'I love you' in my entire life. I responded in a polite way, but still distant, trying to make sense of her message. After a couple of weeks, she asked me if I was going to Portugal that summer in the holidays. I said yes, but that I was going to stay with my friend, Lu. She urged me to at least let Gabriel stay with her. Also, she would love to at least have one day with me, to talk. When the time came, I ended up staying at her house with Gabriel for the night as, the next day, we were going to the Algarve.

I saw a different woman, and she told me about her journey since she left UK. She told me about her hurt, her disappointment with everything I said, and how much it pained her to see that rage in me: so much anger and frustration and she couldn't understand where it was coming from. She told me she'd looked for help as she felt she was in a dark place in her life, but she was feeling better. I knew what she was saying was true; I felt the good energy as soon as she picked us up at airport. It was clean, light and contagious.

On the way home, she told me she always pressured me to continue my studies because she wanted me to have a career and be independent of a man (which I am now). She told me she never said congratulations on my achievements because she knew I was capable of doing so, and even more. In her opinion, people only need congratulations and constant validation if they are stupid, therefore every achievement is a surprise. Nevertheless, she was joyful and proud of me. I understood what she meant; we come from an African culture, where parents are strict and expect you to do well. They will not tell you to your face how proud they are, but they will brag to friends and family about you and your achievements. I learned a long time ago that she is not one to show emotions easily. After we stopped talking, my godmother called me from Angola and told me she would brag about me and all the good things I was doing on my own, even though I was a single mother. She said that when she went to my graduation, she couldn't shut up about how proud she was of me.

So, I accepted what she had to say at that moment. We are from different generations, so I do understand where she comes from. She also told me about her boyfriend and that she was now working, and all the extra activities she had been doing, and I felt very proud of her. That's all I prayed for her: love and a sense of purpose, or at least for her to live the rest of her life in the best possible way. She did apologise for the way things turned out between us, and I apologised as well. What I said in that argument was true, but the way I said it was mean and hurtful, and I do acknowledge that. Sometimes it is not about what you say, but how you say it.

In 2019, I was on my way to Portugal to meet my mother and my sisters, as we were going to Cape Verde in the holidays. My mother organised and paid for the trip, as she wanted to spend some time with us. Who would think that we would ever be on that journey together and willingly? As my mother changed, we all changed, and our relationship with her changed. We became healthier, loving and mature, stopped co-depending on her and became our own individuals, which she is learning to love, respect and celebrate, without trying to constantly change us or criticise. As Wayne Dyer says: 'When you change the way you look at things, the things you look at also change.'

## To my Mother: I chose to love you unconditionally

When I entered therapy, I started a journey. On that journey, I found out things about myself that I was oblivious to. The way I always moved around and related to people is a result of my childhood, of the pain, the shame and the rage I carried around. The way I responded to situations that upset me was related to the rage I was holding on to. Through my journey, I understood that I did love and hate my mother at the same time. I loved her because she was the strongest, most beautiful, compassionate, and kind (to others) woman I knew. She was never able to tell us 'I love you', but she showed me in her own ways, by making sure I had a future, always investing in my studies. She never abandoned me; she was making sacrifices so I could study. I didn't have Portuguese documents, so I couldn't study in the Portuguese private school in Angola, and the public schools weren't safe or reliable. The only alternative was to send me to Portugal. When she put more responsibilities on me, it was because she needed help, because she was tired and, out of all three of us, she knew she could rely on me, that I would do it without making a fuss. When she would shout about everything and nothing, it was because she was frustrated, needed us to understand and give her some peace and quiet or time alone. She was tough on me because she needed me to be tough. She was always afraid of dying and leaving me behind. She knew my sisters had my dad, but would he take care of me if she wasn't around (she told me that herself)?

I hated my mother for what my abuser did to me, for those years I spent in the Algarve and for always thinking she favoured my sisters over me. But that wasn't really fair on her: she was fighting against demons she didn't know existed. I never told her anything that ever happened to me, so how could she try to make it right or at least help me heal? For that I apologise to you, mother, because I know if I had said something, perhaps things could have been different between us. Blaming you without giving you the chance to defend yourself was wrong. But in a way, I thought I was protecting you.

I thought about telling her about Judas so many times, but I feared what she would do. I remember every time there was cases of rapes of children on TV or similar things, she would make some remarks like: 'I would kill the bastard and then hand myself to the police.' I was scared of that, so I kept silent and didn't realise that was the root of every wall between us! I am sorry I kept you in the dark.

Through my journey, and now that I am a mother and have my own struggles, I can understand (although I don't agree with many things) everything she ever did for me and be appreciative of them all. She loved me the way she was taught. She showed me love in the best way she could and knew and did nothing less all her life than provide me with shoes so I could walk. Her way of guidance was at times draining and hurtful, but she had no one in life to show her how to do it from a place of love instead of fear; everything she owned and learned in life was also through pain and hard work. Through my healing, I understood my mother was trying to live her life through me, living her dreams through me, giving me what no one gave her, pressuring me to achieve what she didn't. I realise that, just like me, she also had a child within herself that needed love and empathy. She didn't just stay with my dad for fear of being alone, she stayed until she was sure she could leave with some financial stability for herself, or us, for that matter. She endured suffering, humiliation and betrayal because she didn't want to leave with nothing and let us go into deprivation.

To forgive my mother and accept her with all her flaws, I had to give up my personal history. When you give up your personal history, you have nothing else to live up to. It's like starting over; you become a blank page. You don't forget, but you don't hold on to the past anymore (Wayne Dyer).

From now on I choose to love my mother, admire her and cherish her for all the sacrifices she made for me/us. My mother is the true meaning of the word 'MOTHER'! Therefore, I choose to leave hate, rage and anger behind. I choose to forgive anything I ever held against her and I choose to be as present in her life as I can be. To continue to learn from her, to enjoy moments with her, to see her correcting her motherhood mistakes with her grandchildren, to see her reborn every day like a little baby and enjoying life like she never did before. I choose to be here to teach her new approaches and ways to think in life, to tell her every day that she is worthy, that she is enough, and she is loved (I am sorry no one ever told you that before). Your strength amazes me, your kindness always transcended me, your willingness to learn makes me feel proud of you, and your new way of love teaches me that it's never too late to start over and be happy. You are a true fighter and a true queen. After everything you endured in life, you too made it to the other side, and look at you now! I wish one day to be half of the woman that you are! Thank you for everything you have ever done and continue to do for me and Gabriel – only God knows how much I appreciate you. I LOVE you and I always will.

## To my sisters: I want to be a better big sister

Cape Verde also made me appreciate you as my siblings from a place of love. I had time to get to know you again. Since I've left Portugal, I barely see or talk to you both. When I used to go to Portugal, I used to avoid you because I didn't have the patience to be around you. Being with you always made me feel unsettled and irritated. Any comment would set me off. For many years, I took the title of mean sister (it didn't bother me) because I didn't care for either of you. I did have a connection with Jasmine when she was young, but eventually that got lost as she got older, because she became as lazy and entitled as Vanessa was. Cape Verde brought us together and I can never say thank you enough to mom for making it happen. On our first night there, Vanessa and I stayed awake until 4am talking about our upbringing, our hurts and our messed-up family. I told her about my writing and how it was helping me in my healing process with certain people or events that occurred though my life, and she told me about her struggles with motherhood and married life, and that she too was seeing a therapist, to help her get over her post-partum depression.

My sister is now a grown-up woman, very grounded, humble, loving, wise and considerate. It also came to my attention that I do have something to learn from her: patience. She knows how to remain calm and breathe in chaos, whereas I need a moment to vent and then I seek calmness. I 'met' my sister for the first time, and I enjoyed doing so. We spoke like mature women and sisters from a place of love and with no judgements. We were only able to do it because we left hurt behind and we both chose to move forward with love as a base for everything we do or say to each other.

Jasmine is now on a journey, I understand where she is coming from, but it's difficult to know where she will land based on the decisions she is taking. I respect but I don't agree, but it's not my place to tell her story. She decided to move to the UK and is now living with me. For me it is difficult to see her as a woman; I have to check myself every time I address her. As I said before, she once was my baby girl, and although we grew apart during the years, I never stopped loving my baby or feeling very protective of her (a mother never does). It seems to me she is seeking something that she also doesn't know yet. Nevertheless, I am happy that she felt comfortable enough to ask for my help and support while here in the UK. She is still young and has much to understand as she matures, but at same time she is very resilient, strong-minded, hard-working, funny, caring and trustworthy. I know she will go far and do great in life because, whatever she puts her mind to, she goes to work until she achieves it. I wish I had her strength at her age; I wonder what my life would be right know.

Since we came back from our holidays, I feel a bit depressed. It pains me that, now we all are in a good place with each other, we can't live close so our children can grow together. But I know that where love exists, all things are possible, and we will do our best to be present in each other's lives, as much as we can. Dear sisters, forgive me for all the years I saw you as my enemies and for all the hate and jealousy I felt toward you. Forgive me for not being much of a big sister. I know now you needed me so many times and I wasn't available because I, too, was dealing with my demons. Please accept my love and a promise that I am here to stay. I love you both equally; you are both unique and special to me and I learn so much from you. I'm hoping for us to build many more memories like the ones in Cape Verde. I want more hugs, more happy tears, more laughs, more dancing in the streets, more stupid arguments that end up in a laugh, more sharing, more understanding, more love and more presence. I want to be known by you and I want to know you both. I want to be your big sister and love you exactly as you are.


## To my dad: Help me to forgive you

I love you and appreciate you for everything you've done for me. My real father rejected me, but you raised me as your own. I remember a time that you wanted to give me your name. I remember your disappointment when the solicitor told you that you couldn't. I was sadder for your being than I was for myself. You gave me so much in life but still you took so much. You took my ability to trust men and to love them healthily. I thought Judas did it, but by the time I was a mature woman, I already understood that he was a sick, evil pervert and not all men are like him. As a dad and grandfather, you gave me, and continue to give me and Gabriel, more than I could have ever asked for. As a man, you are everything that I always run away from! It's not my place to talk about my mom's hurt regarding your relationship. But it's my right to tell you about the damage you created in this family. You have done wrong to all of us. Mom was the main victim, but we all suffered. We all came out of your relationship with rage, pain and questions – questions you don't seem willing to answer, that you don't want to hear. They are questions that would help all of us heal, but you don't seem bothered enough to do so! I cannot comprehend how you are almost with a foot in the coffin and still you are unable to ask for forgiveness or apologise for everything that you did. To explain the reasons behind the acts, to give us something that we can hold on to. SOMETHING, Dad – just give us something. I do have love for you, and I do care for you. But I need 'something' more from you; I need you to surrender to the higher power that has been keeping you alive and humble yourself to him and to us. Because, at this point, I can say that I forgive you, but it will not be sincere. However, I promise I will continue to pray for you, asking God to help you in your constant battles with your health and sending you love. Please, please, please open your heart and receive and feel my love; perhaps that will help you ease the internal pain I know you, too, have carried around for so many years. Please, please, please let me understand you, forgive you and move on. I NEED to move on from the enigma that is you. For once, be a considerate human being and show us your vulnerability, and I promise we will meet you halfway.

*Start over; my darling.*

*Be brave enough to find the life you want and courageous enough to chase it. Then start over and love yourself the way you were always meant to.*

- *Madalyn Beck*

# Chapter 3
# Pedro – 'Our paths needed to cross'

Pedro is the father of my child (Gabriel). I met him in an African nightclub in Costa da Caparica, Portugal, around 2006 (more or less). That night he was a pleasant surprise, because I didn't want to go out, but my friend Elisabete asked me to because she needed to clear her head.

I remember seeing him across the room and thinking: 'Damn, who is that dark chocolate over there?' A few years before, he wouldn't even have been my type, as he is really dark. After all the bullying I endured for being black, it's sad to say, but I had a problem dating a man way darker than me. I would start thinking about what our kids would look like and how they would also be bullied at school, and that used to freak me out. Also, secretly, I disliked everything that was too black or too African. But, through my friends Tany, Beto, Victor, Dino, Silo, Herica, Solange, Zuraima, Polonia, Carlinha and Wanderley, I learned to embrace my blackness, to love what black stands for, to appreciate our history and to not be apologetic of who we are or what I am. I finally stopped living in the cross-worlds of not knowing where I belong. As I am light skinned, black folks in Angola did not accept me as black. They did not bully me, but they also wouldn't accept me as black. For them, I was Mulata (not black enough or black with white privileges). However, the white folks at school in Portugal

53

called me negro and bullied me for the colour of my skin. So, for years, I struggled to embrace my blackness or what that represented.

But now I was black! My friends are black, and they are not ashamed of it. They are proud of it, and walk around like some white folks do, with confidence, intelligence. They are ambitious, outspoken and educated. From where I am standing now, they were black excellence in the making. They were my role models; I looked up to them on so many levels, without knowing they taught me a lesson for life. I am black since birth, but I learned to love being black with them. Therefore, I started to look at black people differently, becoming less judgmental, and I started caring less what my family would think of me for dating a dark black man. One thing I also learned is that we black people sometimes are more racist between our kind than white people are with us. I remember when I took Pedro to my family gathering. Most of my family from Angola were in Portugal on holiday, and I thought that would be a good opportunity to introduce him to everyone. On the day, he was well received but, after we left, my auntie said to my mother: 'With so many "good mornings" and "good afternoons", why did Wanuza chose a "midnight"? She is taking our race backwards.'

I was so disappointed and offended that I didn't participate in any more family gatherings. My mother said she didn't mean any harm, and it was a joke. I think differently and, if it was a joke, I wasn't laughing. Before me and Pedro moved in together, our relationship was casual, and on and off for a while. We had no expectations with each other, but we did enjoy each other's company. The first proper date we had was on Valentine's Day and it was super-awkward to sit anywhere and talk about anything.

So, we just went to Nations' Park in Lisbon and walked around while trying to get to know each other. He told me he had two children and was living at his mother's house while trying to get a place for himself, as he and the mother of his children weren't together anymore.

When he told me that, I immediately thought: 'Hmm, two children and living at his mother's? Nah, not for me.' And there I decided we could just be friends or, perhaps, friends with benefits, but definitely not someone for me to have anything serious with. By the end of the night we kissed, but I had no intention of seeing him again. He called me later that day to see if I'd arrived safely at home and then again, after a couple of days, to ask if I was all right. We went out a few more times, and one of the times he took me to his mom's house and introduced me to her and his siblings. That made me feel he was serious about me, and that whatever situations he might have had with baby's mama were resolved. The last thing I wanted was a woman chasing me because I was dating her man. For me it wasn't about the children, it was always about the mother and whatever could still be going on between them. I told him my thoughts and he assured me it was all over. But something was still holding me back, so I was trying to keep it low-key.

One night we went to his sister's for a dinner party and, while talking to her, she made a comment about never understanding her brother's marriage to the woman in question. I asked: 'What brother?' She said: 'Pedro and his wife!' I felt my legs trembling, but I kept it cool because it wasn't the time or place to lose it. After a while I went to Pedro and I told him I wanted to go. In the car I asked him about what his sister said, and he told me he didn't tell me he was married because he was getting a divorce, and he knew I wouldn't believe him (damn right).

After that, I told him that we should stop seeing each other. I was disappointed that he lied about something so simple. I thought he should have given me a chance to choose if I wanted to be with him or not, given his circumstances.

We went our separate ways for a while but kept messaging each other every now and then. On the day he signed his divorce papers, he came and surprised me at my workplace. He asked me if he could take me out for dinner, as he was finally released of his marriage, and the only person he wanted to celebrate was with me. That made me feel special, so I said yes! That same night, we restarted what we'd previously stopped.

For a couple of months, things were great between us. I thought of him as one of my best friends and we could talk about everything. I would help him with his kids when they were around, and his family was actually very nice, and I would spend more time around his family than mine. After three months of being together, he dropped the bombshell that one of his female friends that he got involved with after separating from his wife was pregnant and was going to have the baby soon.

That, for me, was the second red flag! I couldn't continue with him. I had nothing to say to him. I couldn't look at his face, hear his excuses; whatever the explanation was, I wasn't interested in listening to it. I shut down completely. A relationship that starts with constant lies and omissions is doomed to fail from the beginning. I already felt failed in some areas of my life; I didn't need this too. At the time I was looking for a responsible man: faithful, a saviour that would come to save me and make me happy (laugh). I remember asking for that many times in my prayers. As I know now, you need to be careful with what you ask for. I knew I wasn't in love with him, but I was in love with the idea of us. I was in love with the way he cared for his children (most black men with children that I knew where hopeless), with his relationship with his family, the respect and love for his parents, with his loyalty to his friends and his consideration and respect for the mother of his children. The man showed me qualities I hadn't seen in any other black African man. He talked about women with respect and had great family values. For me he was a man, and not the boys I dated before. He is five years older than me, had adult responsibilities, and he acted and took decisions like an adult. Unfortunately, he also lied like an adult.

I wasn't heartbroken, but I was feeling deceived. I asked him not to contact me again. I didn't even want to be his friend because a friend that deceives you has no space in your life. After a week, his sister called me; she wanted to know my version of events which, at the time, I appreciated. We talked for an hour: she told me she understood my point of view, but I had nothing to worry about as he and the new baby's mother had nothing going on. She was positive of what she was saying because she was friends with her. She also told me that he liked me a lot and that she didn't remember seeing him that happy in a long time; and although what he did was wrong, it would be a shame to let it all go without giving it a try.

I gave myself some time to think and, after few days, I called him to meet up. From that point on things became steady. I set the tone and made him understand my standards. If he had anything else to say, now would be the time – I wouldn't give him a third chance. Looking back, I felt like I was in control of our relationship. The fact I wasn't madly

57

in love gave me some sort of power to think I could just jump out if a minimal thing didn't add up or was against whatever ideals I had in my head. Plus, I always had this feeling that me and Pedro had something to achieve together, but that we wouldn't end up together. Don't ask me how, but I knew it. I remember saying to him on numerous occasions: 'I think we are only destined to be good friends. I don't think we are meant to be lovers.' He would laugh, but I was certain of it!

Apart from that, we had a good vibe going on. We were there for each other, enjoyed time together, but we also had a social life apart from each other with our friends, and things were great. At that point, it was the most mature relationship I'd ever had. He was working to achieve his goals (buying his house), I was working during the day and going to university at night, and we were starting to make plans together for the future (after I finished uni). At that point, I was also advising Pedro to go back to education and follow his dream. He mentioned to me that he never had the opportunity to study further because of his circumstances and, when he had, his wife didn't support him. So, I felt sorry for him. I could see so much potential, but too little opportunity, and I started feeling compelled to be that woman that would take him further, give him that push in life he needed. I told him that we were together in this fight and I would support him in anything he needed to start the studies and achieve his dreams.

## Coming to terms with grief

Not long after we started making plans and working on them, I got pregnant! I couldn't remember feeling that scared in a long time. I know my body so well that, even before the test, I knew I was pregnant. I woke up one morning and I felt different; my body felt strange. At night when I spoke to him, I told him I was pregnant. He asked me if I did the test, and I said no, but I was 100 per cent sure. Then I said: 'I am not having it!' He said he would support me in whatever decision I took.

The next day, on the way to work, I stopped at a pharmacy and took a pregnancy test. The results were positive, as I anticipated. I called him straight away to give him the news. He was silent for a bit, then asked me: 'What do you want to do?'

I said: 'I told you already that I am not having it! Although it takes two to tango, I should have been more responsible with my pill (I would miss it for two days and then take them together, etc). Plus, I am still studying, I work part-time, I live with my parents, I am not ready to be anyone's mother, you already have three children, are still living with your mother, have very insecure work and our relationship is not strong enough to make me wonder, 'what if'. Did I miss anything?'

He said: 'No. But I don't know if you are aware: abortions in Portugal are illegal! I know there are places we can go, but I don't know the conditions, and it's normally around €750. We also have the option to go to Spain so you can do it in better conditions, but it will be even more expensive. We will need money for transport, accommodation and to pay the clinic.'

For the first time, I stopped to think about the gravity of the situation! How the hell did I let myself get into this mess? I heard about young girls having abortions in these clinics and then dying of blood loss or getting severe infections and not being able to have any more children. Adding to that was the risk of the authorities finding out and prosecuting me for it. I couldn't breathe. I couldn't think. I was exasperated. What was I supposed to do?

59

I said to Pedro: 'I've got to go. I will talk to you later.'

When I got to work, my colleague saw me come into the shop and followed me to the dressing room. I told her what happened, and she gave me a few minutes to compose myself. I lay down on the sofa we had in our lunchroom and I cried my stupidity and fear away. I asked God for forgiveness for being heartless, but I could not have this child now: it wasn't my time, and it wasn't that child's time. I asked for forgiveness to perhaps go against God's plans, but just this time. I was pretty much sure the decision was mine that, given my circumstances, I had the right to not want to bring this child into the mess my life was. I told God I knew it was my fault; I should be more careful. I owned it and regretted being so careless but asked Him to please not punish me further as the guilt I was feeling was already punishment enough.

When I finally managed to get down to the shop floor for my shift, I saw one of the pharmacists from the place where I did my pregnancy test. I approached her as she was also my regular customer and asked her how I could help her. She looked at me and said: 'Sorry if I am being intrusive. Please don't get offended. I am here to help; you can trust me!'

I said: 'OK!'

She proceeded: 'Are you happy with the results?'

I responded: 'Not at all!'

She asked: 'What are you going to do?'

I said: 'I don't want to have it, but I will need money to go away: Spain maybe.'

Then she said: 'I can help. Come to see me at 1 p.m., but don't tell anyone.'

I was so desperate and curious that I didn't think – I just went! We met in the middle of the street in a dodgy corner of the city. She told me again that she just wanted to help me. When I asked why, she said: 'You've always been nice to me, and you give me your forty per cent discount every time I shop with you, or reserve things for me more times than you are allowed. You do not have to do that, but you do. A person that is generous to strangers demonstrates kindness, and I appreciate that. So, let it be me helping you this time. But I need to know that I can trust you, as I could lose my credentials and be arrested over this.'

I was so desperate that I didn't ask questions: I just said of course (and I meant it). She told me about some pills meant for stomach ulcers or something like that but, when applied to the vagina while pregnant, they caused contractions and miscarriage. She said she'd used it before and most women that work in clinics or hospitals use it too as it's 'easier, clean, fast, less painful and a silent' way of doing an abortion. I asked her how much that would be, and she said only €10.

I asked if she wanted any more money for it? She said: 'No, Aurea! I have a daughter your age. I'd rather you did it with me in a controlling way than go somewhere else and put yourself in danger. I've already spoke to my colleague at the counter. She will dispense you the pills, you pay her directly like any other prescription and then apply two pills tonight. If something goes wrong and you end up in the hospital, pretend you didn't know you were pregnant, and they will class it as a miscarriage. Whatever you do, please do not mention my name or my workplace.'

I agreed with everything, got to the pharmacy, bought the pills and went back to the shop to finish my shift.

I called Pedro and told him what happened. He sounded awfully happy with the news, and never asked me if I wanted him to be with me, to hold my hand, comfort me, nothing at all. All I got at the end of the call was a 'let me know how it goes', like I was going to my last exam at school or something. That made me feel more sure that I was making the right decision, and that men are self-centred creatures that only think about themselves. I felt disgusted with his attitude, but I had bigger things to worry about than him.

That afternoon, I didn't go to university, but went straight home. As soon as I was home, I put on my pyjamas, introduced the pills and went to bed around 8 p.m. By 10 p.m. I started feeling strong pains which I thought were stomach pains, but I know now were contractions. I lay down in my bed in agony, holding my belly tight in a foetal position and with a pillow on my face so no one could hear me crying in pain and resentment for myself. After an hour or so, I felt an urgent need to pee. I rushed to the toilet and what felt like a bag full of water came out of me (if I can describe it like that). I looked down and there was blood everywhere, but I couldn't see anything. I flushed the toilet straight away in panic of someone coming in and because I was feeling sick with so much blood. I cleaned myself and went back to bed.

I didn't sleep much that night. I lay down still and looked at the ceiling for a long time while tears came down from my eyes. I remember feeling relieved and guilty at same time, thinking that I was a horrible human being, that perhaps I was deserving of everything bad that ever happened to me. I didn't pray that night and for a while after, because I was ashamed of myself. I was trying to process everything, and I was struggling to come to terms with what I did. Just because I decided from the beginning that I didn't want to have that child didn't make it easier to come to terms with the abortion.

The next day, I went to work like nothing happened. I was bleeding heavily and had to drive to work instead of taking public transport. My colleague came to me and asked me what happened as I was looking pale, numb and tired. I told her everything and she told me I should be home resting and not there doing an eight-hour shift. But I couldn't be at home with my mother and my sisters; I needed somewhere quiet to stay but, since I didn't have that I preferred to be at work. We came to an agreement that I would go to the staff room to lie down every time I felt the need.

Straight after we opened the shop, the pharmacist came over to check on me. She asked me how I was and how everything went. I told her about the pain and the toilet incident, and she said I had contractions, and what felt like a bag was the foetus coming out. I felt sick to my stomach again! She then told me I would be bleeding for a month, but it was normal as long it wasn't heavy bleeding for thirty days. Then she made me promise I would make an appointment at the women's clinic to make sure everything was clear.

Before she left, she asked me again: 'How do you feel, hun?'

I started crying and said I felt like a monster and didn't even know why, because I didn't want to have a baby.

She said: 'Aurea, that's life. Just because you thought that was the best thing to do given your circumstances, it does not mean that the aftermath will be easier. I call it adult life! I have a friend who is a psychologist. If you want, I can refer you to her; she will be happy to help you if you want.'

I said thank you, but I would be OK; I just needed time to process and move on. She gave me her number in case it was needed and then left. A total stranger was more concerned about me than the supposed person I was in a relationship with. Pedro didn't call me until he finished his shift at work that day. That night, I missed uni again and went straight home to my bed. He called and called, and I didn't answer until the next morning. I saw all his missed calls and text messages and then I replied: 'The issue is resolved! You can breathe now and leave me alone.'

That day, I decided to stay home and called in sick. I stayed in bed all day. My mother was home so I told her I was having period cramps so she would leave me alone. For six months, I shut down completely: I stopped seeing Pedro and missed loads of classes at uni, so I started struggling to keep up with assignments. My life was literally home to work, work to home and, when home, lying on my bed staring at the ceiling. I lost weight and I would avoid being around my friends. At work I would pretend I was all right and laugh. At home the climate between me and my family wasn't great, but I had nowhere to go and didn't want to talk with anyone either. I was a prisoner to my thoughts: I felt like, during those months, I lost my will to do anything. I was blank, empty, had nothing inside zero, nada, completely numb. Even my mother asked me one time if I was alright. When I asked why, she said: 'You look like you are going to crack any time. What's the matter? Your boyfriend left you?'

To that I smiled cynically and said: 'No, all good. Just too much going on at uni and work. I'm tired, that's all.'

One day, I dreamed about Pedro. In my dream he said: 'We have unfinished business; our story hasn't finished yet.' I didn't really pay much attention to it. Normally I tend to act on my dreams, but I wasn't ready to see him. Looking at him was difficult, plus I felt like he'd failed me when I most needed him. I thought he was different, but apparently, he wasn't.

Six months passed, and I received a text from him asking how I was and saying he'd finally got the keys to his house. He was going to throw a party to inaugurate it on the Saturday of that week and said it would be nice to see me there. It's nothing fancy, he said, just lunch with friends until late, so you can come after work. At the end he said: 'I miss you'.

I didn't reply, but I mentioned it to a mutual friend of ours (Angela) from work. She said I should consider going, then perhaps talk to him to tell him exactly how I felt about everything that had happened. I said: 'I don't owe him anything!'

She replied: 'You owe it to yourself. You are not the same person since everything happened. You walk around with a big dark cloud over your head. Just go and tell him. After that, see how you feel and move forward from there.'

Saturday, I left work with the intention of going home. I completely forgot about the party. When I got home, I parked the car and, when leaving it to get into the building, I suddenly remembered. So, I got back into the car and drove to his house. When I got there, I stayed in the car trying to decide if I should go in or not! By the time I decided to ring the bell, he was coming out with a friend from work. We stared at each other, not knowing what to say. I then said hi to his friend, we talked for a little bit and then she left. Now it was just me and him and an awkward silence. 'I wasn't expecting you anymore,' he said.

'I wasn't coming, then I forgot about it, and now here I am,' I said.

We stayed there looking at each other awkwardly, until he invited me to go in. He showed me around the house, we talked about his kids and some other random things, but then out of the blue he asked me: 'So, what happened to you? You disappeared?'

'Funny you asking me that! Where were you when I needed you? I don't remember you offering me your help or checking on me. You let me go home and do the abortion on my own, and on the next day you called me after your shift finished. Your actions told me everything I needed to know. So, I withdrew myself from your life because it was clear there was no space for me there.'

He said: 'That's not true! From the beginning you acted like everything was under control and my opinion didn't matter on anything. I understand it's your body and the last word should always be yours, but I felt like perhaps you wanted space, and having me asking questions and wanting to know your every move would upset you. You are difficult to read and please. Given the circumstances, I thought giving you space was the best way to go. Maybe I should have been more thoughtful, but I honestly didn't know what to do or what to say. I was as lost and afraid as you were, but I didn't think I had the right to manifest anything because as much as I was feeling that way, I know you were feeling ten thousand times worse.'

We sat in his kitchen in silence for a while until he said: 'Listen, I'm sorry I wasn't there for you!'

And I said: 'I am sorry I shut you down!'

We hugged for a bit, and I felt like a heavy weight was pulled out of my chest. Talking to him didn't change what happened, but Angela was right: it gave me the closure I needed. We talked some more about what happened, and what had happened to me and him in those past six months we hadn't seen each other, until we got tired and went to bed. Sleeping beside him with his arms around me made me feel overwhelmed: I felt like my spirit came back to my body, felt warm again, like a human being and not a cold, heartless bitch. I felt light again and ready to move on from my grief.

*'We cannot start over, but we can create a new beginning.'*
*– Zig Ziglar*

## My green card to Freedom

When Pedro and I decided to move in together, for me it was a spur-of-the-moment decision. I was tired of the life I had at home with my family and he offered me the perfect solution for my problems. Since this letter is for my own healing experience, I must be honest, and the truth is that the moment he asked me to move in, I realised that he loved me, but I … I didn't love him … I liked him, adored him, respected him, and before everything, I thought of him as my best friend. I thought we had the perfect ingredients for a good and promising relationship. As selfish as it might sound, I saw an opportunity and I took it. I saw him as my saviour, the one that gave me a place to be me, to be happy and to finally breathe.

When the recession hit harder in 2008, Pedro and I decided to leave after I got my Portuguese citizenship. We couldn't leave earlier as I was illegal at the time: my immigration paper status expired. I didn't think I had to renew it as I had already applied for the Portuguese citizenship. I was also working and studying, so I felt safe. In the meantime, I was made redundant and couldn't apply for new jobs or ask for Jobseeker's Allowance with no documentation. I had to look for cleaning jobs and live in fear that if the immigration services or the police caught me, I would be deported. At the same time, Pedro's company went into administration and he too was out of a job and taking any jobs that came his way. It was hard: for months we would pay for everything and, by the 15th of the month, we wouldn't even have €1 in our accounts to buy bread. I remember many times asking my friend Tany for money, to get things until the end of the month. Although I see Tany as my big brother, those were humiliating times. One thing I always hated was to ask for money or anything else, from whoever.

Eventually, things turned around. When I received a notification of my citizenship, we waited until the end of the month to go do my ID. At the same time, my friend Wanderley was already living in London, so I spoke to him. I told him about our situation and that me and Pedro were wondering about going to the UK. Straight away, he told me we could both go and stay at his house. He said his wife was working in a factory and they needed people. So, there was a good chance of us getting jobs quickly. He also said: 'I will buy your tickets for the 4th of August, that will give you time to do your ID. Make sure you pay for the advance service so you can receive it on the same day.' I remember saying to him: 'You don't have to pay for our tickets, you know?'

And he said: 'I know! But I want to. Just get your ass over here; your time in Portugal is over. Better opportunities are waiting for you over here.'

I laughed and told him I would pay him with interest. From that point, things moved forward quickly. Pedro put the house with an agency to rent and, by some miracle, in the same week we had two lads interested in it. Because we were running out of time, he had to give full power to my mother to represent him in court lawfully. We packed all our things, said our goodbyes to family and close friends, and ventured together to an unknown future.

Life in London was strange and funny. The area where we were living (Middlesex/Heathrow) seemed nothing like the UK. Although I am foreign myself, I found it funny that I could not see too many white English. Everything around me was foreign: languages, shops and people. People looked guarded and cold in their approach. Everything was rushed, aggressive and impatient. I found myself many times feeling slow and stupid while moving among people.

I had two jobs during the week. One was at a clothes warehouse from 6 a.m. – 3 p.m. (with Pedro), and an office cleaning job from 5 – 9 p.m. Both jobs were well paid, but life in London was so expensive that me and Pedro concluded we probably would need to have two more jobs each to have a decent life. Also, we decided before we moved to the UK that the main reason we wanted to move abroad, was education. We wouldn't be able to study in London while having four jobs each. That's when we decided to move to Wolverhampton. Pedro's younger brother, Miguel, had been living there for a couple of years, so the transition was smooth. Pedro moved first, as his brother managed to get him a place in the car warehouse where he was working (Denso). After a month, he managed to get us a flat in the same building where Miguel was living, and I too moved to Wolverhampton. I remember my friend Wanderley being apprehensive about me leaving to go to a place where I had no friends or family.

'If things do not work out, make sure you come back here. With Pedro or without Pedro, you come back here! All right?'

'All right! Thank you hun for everything; you are out of this world. God bless you and your family always! I know we've already paid you for the tickets, but what you've done for us has no price. I don't know how I will ever be able to repay your kindness.'

We hugged tight and he said: 'Kindness is paid with kindness. If you ever see someone in need, be kind to them, and we will be even.' That is Wanderley: one of the sweetest souls I have ever met!

Wolverhampton was my true welcome as a foreign person in the UK and life experience in partnership with Pedro. I took a week to adapt, rest and put my thoughts in the right place.

After that, I started looking for jobs and ended up at Magna, a chocolate factory in Telford. In the meantime, Pedro decided to swap jobs and start with me at this factory. Our shifts were Thursday, Friday and Saturday from 7.30 a.m. – 7.30 p.m., working on the line doing the same thing over and over again for twelve hours. We had supervisors that talked to us like we were low-life people, ignorant and stupid. On the other hand, the people working with us would constantly tell me to let Pedro work and I should be home having children after children and claiming benefits. I was too pretty to be there, and that was the way English society worked. I felt like I was dying (mentally) slowly at that job. I started wondering what kind of country we had landed in – not even people in Africa have that mentality anymore (at least, not in big cities). I used to cry all the way to the factory until starting my shift – that's how much I hated the job.

I told Pedro I was going to either go crazy or go back to my mother's house. I couldn't stay there any longer. I remember thinking many times a day, every time I was working: 'This is not my destination; this is just the way.' I refused to think that I left Portugal for that kind of job. It's honest work, but I knew and I felt that that wasn't my calling; there was more for me out there. We both started looking for other jobs on our days off but, as recession also hit the UK, it started to be more difficult to get good jobs without an English certificate or higher education, and we were both tired of warehouse jobs with minimal pay (or less than that). So, we both enrolled to do English lessons at school, to improve our English and to be able to apply to university when the time came.

One day, we went to do our shifts and were told we had been made redundant as the factory was going to close early for the holidays because it was too hot to produce chocolate (apparently, it alters the consistency of the product). 'What now?' I thought. Both of us unemployed seemed like a nightmare that I wanted to wake up from it even before it started. I remember going to the job centre, seeing people arguing with the advisers, some advisers treating some customers like criminals and me thinking that I didn't want to be there. I didn't want to be another number, go there every two weeks and perhaps be treated as badly as some of the people I had seen. I understood things were changing politically in the country; I was an immigrant in Portugal as well and I understood the best way of staying out of government's way was to work, pay taxes and stay within the law. That was clear to me from the beginning, but not so much for Pedro.

We did apply for Jobseeker's Allowance because we needed to. I was never paid it, but Pedro was, so he started being picky about jobs. I remember asking our landlord (Chris) if he could get us jobs in his friend's hotel, otherwise it would be difficult moving forward to pay him the rent on time. The same day, he called me to say I could go the next day for a trial as a housekeeper. Chris was our saviour during those times. When we were unemployed, struggling with money and barely had enough to eat, I told Chris that we could only pay half the rent until we received Housing Benefit. Instead of getting mad, he let us stay there for free for two weeks and got me the job at the Connaught Hotel. When Pedro started receiving his benefits and me my salary, I tried to pay him the late money, but he wouldn't accept it (another Angel in my life; thank you Chris, may your soul rest in peace).

Given the circumstances, I was expecting Pedro to step up as a man and move heaven and earth to find a job and help me support the house. But, instead, the man started having entitlement syndrome. He thought that, because he was receiving benefits, why should he get just any job? I remember saying to him: 'So you can't do any kind of work, but I can? I also moved here to look for better opportunities, but I am cleaning people's shit. Do you think I like that? Ah, and don't forget that I am more educated than you are. But I understand that we need to start somewhere.'

But it was like talking to a wall, so eventually I just let him be. Meanwhile, I started working on my future. I knew I wanted to finish the tourism course I started in the university in Portugal. Therefore, I enrolled myself in some courses in college: I was doing French, Italian, Spanish and English during the day (after work) at Paget Road College, and an Airport Passenger Assistant Course at night at Metro College in Wolverhampton. I didn't like my job, but the fact I was studying gave me motivation to keep going. I focused so much on that; Pedro became almost invisible to me.

Anyway, everything in him would annoy me. I wasn't used to seeing a grown man sitting on his ass at home while the woman would go to work. My dad had many flaws, but I never saw him take a day off work, not even when sick – he would always go to work. So, Pedro's behaviour was definitely a turn-off for me.

My sister Vanessa came to stay with us for a while after a year of living in the UK, and she also made remarks about Pedro's behaviour. I remember her saying to me: 'So he is the one with children and you are the one working to feed them? Also, you are educated, so why are you here doing cleaning? You're better off in Angola; Dad can get you a good job and a better life than this!'

I responded: 'I am focusing on myself and I couldn't care less about Pedro. At the moment, he is on benefits, but soon that finishes. I am not going to support his lazy ass. Regarding Angola, I am too Western already to live in a corrupted country like that. Don't worry, I know what I am doing, and I have a feeling that I am where I am supposed to be.'

## A disappointment of a men

After six months, Pedro's benefits were stopped, and things became a bit more off between us. Now I was fully supporting the house financially, and I wasn't happy about it. If you see your man trying and fighting, you sure feel like you should have his back, but that wasn't the case! Things became even worse when I found some conversations between him and an ex of his on our laptop. The conversation wasn't anything deep, but the tone was disrespectful, and I could see that he was trying to open a door with no return. I felt enraged!

Oh boy, that fool was playing with the wrong girl. If he thought that, just because I was there on my own, he was going to play me like I was stupid, he sure didn't know me. I showed the conversations to him and told him that he could pack his stuff and go and give the kisses to his friend in person. Perhaps she would love to have his parasite ass living with her, as I sure was tired of him. I said he was a low-life man living at my expense and trying to play me. He didn't say anything, but left and went to his brother, who lived downstairs. I noticed he left his keys, so I packed some of his stuff, put it on the stairs and locked him out.

You want to play me – I will tell you who plays better, I thought.

Then I called my friend Elisabete and told her what was going on. Straight away she told me: 'As soon you finish your courses at the college, move over here. You are too isolated over there.' Yes, she was right, I was. I could also go back to London but, although I loved Wanderley, London's life wasn't my cup of tea. I decided that, as soon as August came, I was going to move with my friend to Bournemouth. I'd had enough of being there living with this ungrateful man. Next day, when I was coming home from work, he stopped me at the stairs and asked me if we could talk, to which I replied: 'I have nothing to say to you! If what you want is to move back in, then you have two days to find a job and stick to it. Then I will think about talking to you. Also, I think I was very specific from the beginning of our relationship that I don't do cheating or betrayal. You want to go kiss or have sex with other women, then go. It's not even like our sex life is amazing anyway. I can't even look at you that way because I do not respect you as a man anymore. You stay home all day. I go to work, you are asleep. I come home from work, you are sitting in your pyjamas telling me you are looking for jobs online, when the truth is you are talking with girls! FOR REAL? Boy, please get out of my way, I don't have time for bullshit.'

Again, he had nothing to say. After two days, Miguel came to intervene for his brother, asking me to let him at least sleep on the sofa as he didn't have space to have his brother around. Once again, I said: 'When he gets a job, he can move in.' That same day, Pedro told me he got a job at the hotel as a waiter. I let him move in and sleep on the sofa but didn't talk to him for weeks. I was done; I had my plans, and I was going to be out of there as soon as possible.

The thing with me and Pedro is that, even in our low moments, we always had our friendship. So, no matter what, we always managed to eventually talk through our differences. After a while, things became steady between us. I let go of my idea of moving to Bournemouth. My sister Jasmine moved to the UK because she wanted to live with me and study art here. I got pregnant and we finally got the council house we'd been waiting two years for. One thing I must give to Pedro: he was good at taking care of all the paperwork (at least, I thought so), like taxes, council tax, bank, etc. I always felt that was his department; I didn't understand English laws and could not be bothered with that (which was a big mistake).

*Never allow waiting to become a habit. Live your dreams and take risks. Life is happening now.*

*– Paulo Coelho –*

My pregnancy came as a surprise to everyone (because I'd applied to university), but not to us. I (we) planned every step of the way. I cannot explain, but I knew that was the way to go for me. Apply to uni, get pregnant and do my degree while on maternity leave from work (at least the first year), and the other two years while Gabriel was still in the nursery for a couple of hours.

And that's exactly what happened. I was four months pregnant when I went to do my English exams at uni and find out if I was able to start in September. After two weeks I received my results, and I was in – we both were (me and Pedro). Pedro got in at Wolverhampton University doing Business Management and I got in at UCB, Birmingham, doing Tourism Business Management. By the time the classes started, I was on maternity leave and heavily pregnant.

My first day at uni, I moved around like a pregnant elephant, was tired all the time, and fell asleep at the introductory classes. That day I went home, talked to Pedro and told him that I was not sure if I should wait another year, as I'd underestimated how hard it could be to do all this at the same time. His response, however, upset me to my core: 'I think I should do it first while you stay home with Gabriel and continue with your work part-time, and then when I finish and find a better job, that can help pay for the bills, then you can do your degree!'

I laughed, but I didn't say anything. All I thought was: 'What if it doesn't happen straight away for you? What shall I do? Wait until your magic happens and then I can go and do mine? Nah, I'm thirty next year with a child on the way – that's not an option. As much as it might sound crazy, I was feeling my calling, and I wasn't going to put that on hold for much longer. That was my moment, I was sure about it, and I was going to act on it. But I also wanted to enjoy my last months of pregnancy and rest. The next day, I went to see my course manager at university, to explain my situation, and she advised me that since my baby was going to be born in December, I could start in February if I really didn't want to wait until September. I called my mother and she told me that I should go for it. She said that, nowadays, having kids doesn't stop anyone. It can make it harder to achieve things, but it doesn't stop you. I told her what Pedro said and she said: 'If you are willing to wait another three years, then go for it!'

No, I wasn't, so I went to the office and made a referral to start in February, then stayed home for the next three months preparing for our baby's arrival. My sister Jasmine eventually decided to go back to Portugal, and that was a relief for us: I wasn't ready to take care of a teenager.

*An Arrow Can only be shot by pulling it backward. So, when life is dragging you back with difficulties, it means that it's going to launch you into something great.*

- *Paulo Coelho*

## What are your Priorities?

Fast forward three years, and Pedro decided to go to Angola after he finished his degree. Most people from our background did the same, and they were doing well over there. So, he thought that this was his chance to go and do well for him and his family. We talked about it and, at the beginning, he was only going for holidays and to reconnect with his motherland to see if things were really as people were telling us. We're both Angolan, but I left there when I was eleven years old, and Pedro when he was three. I went back again in 1997 for the Easter holidays, but Pedro never put his foot back there. Whatever he knew from his birth country was passed on to him; he never experienced Angola for himself. I always supported him in the idea of getting to know his country of birth; I am a firm believer that for people like us we should try to know, explore and reconnect with our roots. I believe that reconnecting to your roots is something necessary to every individual. It helps you understand your inner self, your beliefs, hopes and aspirations in life. It is in our DNA, and if you understand the external, perhaps you can understand the internal and 'grow' from that.

So, I pushed him to go. This was also one of his dreams, and I always thought that a good partner doesn't get in the way of the other. Instead, you support and push them to keep going when they feel things are getting hard. However, the agreement between us was that he would go for a month or so, to see if what people were saying was right (in terms of opportunities). The war had been finished for twelve years and Angola was developing in many areas. People were often saying that the money was there, that Angola was 'the new Dubai'.

But I know my country, so I kept my guard high (until now). In a country with so much corruption and so much social inequality, how could you say it was the new Dubai? Also, I had a child, and I was not taking my son to a place where he would have to have many immunisation injections to be safe. Don't get me wrong, I love and I miss Angola as it's part of me. I would have gone there on holidays more often if it wasn't too expensive. Also, with a tourism degree, I would have even better prospects, as my father has connections with some people in the government. But that's the thing: if you tell me a country is developing, I need to see social equality starting with things that we take for granted in the Western world, like water and electricity for everyone, healthcare and education provided by the government at an affordable price and opportunities for everyone, not just for some individuals because their father happens to be friends with the highest figures in the country. Some people call me idealist, but I don't think I'm in the wrong here.

Pedro was very enthusiastic about the idea of going on holiday, and I was happy for him. But everything changed when his father came to spend Christmas with us. At the beginning, I was quite happy to have his father at our house; Gabriel never had a proper relationship with him, and this was the opportunity for that. Plus, I grew up with the desire to create a perfect family (there is no such thing), with reasonable and strong moral values, maybe because mine was a mess! After a while, his father started to annoy me with his chauvinism and sense of entitlement. He demanded things like he was the one paying bills: 'Oh, I don't drink that cheap whiskey as it gives me a headache. You better buy me the good one. – are you going out? Don't forget to bring me that wine I like. Are we eating the same food from yesterday? I don't like leftovers.'

Bear in mind that at this point the only one working in the house was Pedro. I would do some cleaning at people's houses now and then but, with both of us at uni and Gabriel, there were only so many hours me and him could work. We were depending on housing benefit to help with half of the rent, and for those three years we were living on the minimum necessary. On top of his remarks, he used to talk to his son like I wasn't there, telling him things like: 'When I was your age, I had many girlfriends; I don't know from you and your brothers who takes after me. Why are you going to Angola on holiday? You should go, find a job and stay there, if Wanuza then decides to go, good; but if not, you are young and you can build a family there and still have this one here for when you come on holiday.'

'Is this man for real?' I asked myself. And why the hell is Pedro not saying anything? Does he want me to start breaking stuff around the house to get his attention and tell him his father is going too far and being disrespectful? 'Breathe in, breathe out.'

His father wasn't my problem: I didn't live with him or have a child with him. He owes me nothing apart from respect, but that generation of African man can be chauvinists, selfish and inconsiderate in their actions and remarks. I decided I would deal with Pedro when the time was right and ignore his father for the time being.

Two days before Christmas, while we were going to town for some shopping, Pedro said: 'I was thinking about what my dad said, and since I've already spent the savings on the flight ticket, I think if I find a job there, I should just stay there, and then you and Gabriel could come and join me. You can come after your graduation or when you feel prepared to move over there. What do you think?' He asked me!

I thought: 'WHAT DO I THINK? What do I think, he asks me, after the many conversations we had about this subject? After we made an agreement as a COUPLE and decided that we would stay here, maybe move to London or

Bournemouth after he comes back from Angola. What do I think, he asks me? I think that you should go to hell and leave me alone, that's what I think!' But my words were: 'I am not changing my mind; I am not going back to Angola. Holidays? Maybe! But living there is out of question, especially with a child. Now you do what you think is best for you and your family!' He went quiet!

Then I said: 'Since we are having this conversation, let me tell you something: you better have a word with your father, because the next time he disrespects me in my house and you sit there without saying anything, the house will come down! I don't allow people in my family to disrespect you. I always try to make sure that they understand they don't have to like you but have to respect you, so I expect the same from your side.'

'Just ignore him. It's a different generation and sometimes they can be over the top. You know how he is!'

'No! You don't understand. It's my house – from the moment he steps in, he owes me respect. I don't give a shit if he is older or not: respect goes both ways. You better have a word with him, because if I open my mouth it won't be pretty. Then don't go tell people that I have a bad temper or that I am crazy. I promise you, Pedro, it won't be difficult for me to make him understand the basics of RESPECT.'

'I will have a word with him later today when we go to see Miguel. Until then, just chill, please!'

I thought: 'CHILL? What the hell do you think I have been doing these last two weeks? Jumping up and down full of joy like a monkey? Let your father disrespect me one more time and you will see the blackness coming out of me. I will give you both "CHILL". You don't tell a black woman to chill when she is boiling inside. He should know that by now!'

We had already been growing apart for years, the uni days just made it clearer to me. I was always very supportive of whatever dreams Pedro had, but I didn't feel the same from him. It was always like he came first: his needs first, his dreams first, his family first. His way of thinking was a bit backward sometimes, and I couldn't understand how someone that was now in uni could also be so ignorant and small-minded in certain things. I also noticed that, now that I wasn't working, that he would make constant comments about how I had to find a stable job to help more. This was coming from a man that stayed unemployed for two years because he thought he was too good for jobs like cleaning and working in a warehouse.

After our conversation in the car, it became more annoying for me to listen to him talking about his trip to Angola with other people. He was so caught up in his own dream that he couldn't see that we were drifting apart. The more I tried not to think about it, the more I realised I wasn't up to dealing with this relationship anymore.

However, I had a lot on my plate, so I just thought that probably stress was winning me over. I had a dissertation to finish, my last university exams, was starting to panic with the idea of finishing uni and probably having to go on benefits (I couldn't bear the thought).

Christmas that year was at our friends' house (Tuxa and Ray). All night the conversation was all about Angola. At one point, Tuxa said: 'Well, if the money is in Angola, maybe now you will be able to give Wanuza the wedding she deserves. So many years together I think it's time; you won't find another woman like her!'

Pedro went quiet, looking at me with pity eyes. At the end of the night, Vanessa and I went upstairs to talk, and I told her that during our last holidays in Portugal he proposed to me, but I didn't accept it.

She asked: 'Why not? Are you waiting for years?'

'Exactly. He had a million chances to do so! But now he realised I am not fighting for this relationship anymore, he thinks that I deserved it? What about when I was there for him in every corner supporting him through all his arguments with his baby's mothers, taking care of his children like mine, working for the family while he was unemployed. I lost myself in this relationship to make it work for us, because that's what couples do (or so I thought); especially after Gabriel, I was willing to stay no matter what because, for me, it's family before anything else. For What? This man is the most selfish person that I know even his mum agrees with me. Ah, and on top of it, the constant disrespect from his father, and the only thing he says is: 'Just ignore him.' I am his partner; a good husband should profess, protect and provide for his woman and family (Steve Harvey). If I wasn't worthy after all these years of a wedding, then I am sure that I am not now either, because I don't give a shit anymore. I am telling you, Tuxa, I will finish uni and find a job, I guarantee you, and if he wants to stay in Angola, that's it, I am done with him. If he decides to come back, things will have to change around here. He will have to prove himself to me, that he is worthy of me. I can't deal with his selfishness anymore. He is in love with the family picture he carries around to show to everyone. For a while I too was in love with the idea of us, but it is time to be real – we are not kids anymore. Do not get me wrong, if he has money, he is really sweet and buys me things, but he always makes sure that people can see his good actions so that he can come across as the perfect partner.

Eight years together; I know him inside out, but you ask him questions about me, and I guarantee you that he knows nothing about me. This man doesn't know me at all. I am not doing this anymore; there are two in this relationship, plus Gabriel. My ambitions are as important as his are. Time to start thinking a little bit about myself. He can follow me, or he can go find another dumb woman that is willing to stay eight years with him dreaming about wonderland.'

'Wow. Seems like you are carrying a big, heavy bag full of frustration, disappointment and resentment around with you! Did you guys talk about it?'

'Yes. Well, I talk, and he listens! Pedro doesn't talk he is a caveman. For him, everything is just fine. He can see that I am not happy the way things are, but he will leave it to escalate to a point of no return. I know I have a difficult personality, but if something is wrong, I need to talk. If he is not talking, then I shut down. Also, he thinks that everything can be solved with sex. I know that he has already made his mind up about staying in Angola, but he will pretend that it was a last-minute decision and a hard one to make. You will see!'

'Yes, men are like that. They think that we are like them that we use our vaginas to think. Of course, we also have needs like they have, but we are more rational than that. But I must tell you, I am amazed and surprised with everything that you just told me. For all of us, you guys are just perfect together – always synchronised with everything, it's like you are soulmates! I guess that what people say is right: "Behind closed doors, only you know what's going on inside your house."

'We look like the perfect couple because, during these years, I thought that I owed that to him!'

'Owe him? What do you mean?' Tuxa asked me, puzzled.

'I think I told you before that I always had a troubled relationship with my mom. Living with her was always toxic. When I met Pedro, me and my mother were at breaking point and I needed to get out of her house. When I went to live with him at his house, it felt like coming out of jail. That was one of the happiest moments of my life, and I felt I owed it to Pedro. Hence why I felt, all these years, that it was my obligation to make things work, to be here for the good and the bad. I would put my foot down on things that I didn't like, but I was here for the long run. But now ... nah, I think I paid my price.'

Tuxa was looking at me. All she said was: 'Whatever happens, I am here for you! But you are right, it's not healthy to be in a relationship feeling like this. Make sure that, before he goes, you two sit and put things in black and white. I feel sad for both of you as I like to see you two together. But I guess you know what is best for you, and no one has the right to give much opinion on your relationship.'

The party season went well as we spent it at Tuxa's house. She was my rock during those tough times with Pedro. Although she was twenty-five at the time, she was also more mature than most women I knew. Tuxa is a 'positivity energy' person. She is funny, happy, wise, intelligent, honest, truthful, strong, ambitious and a friend of her friends. I could be having the worst day of my life, but a word with her and my mood would change in five seconds. I honestly think that she has an old soul inside of her, because she gives advice like a wise grandmother or mother would give it to you. She is the type of friend that will tell it as it is: if you are fat you are, if you look beautiful, she will compliment you, if she thinks you should be running for president, she will make your headache until you run the damn campaign. Even when she is down, we always end up having a laugh, the sort that makes your stomach-ache.

I used to often ask her for advice, as I was very impulsive and explosive at times! She is calmer than me and would put me in my place if she saw I was overreacting or reading too much into things. Talking to her always calms me down and helps me see things from a different perspective. And the fact that she is married also helps, as she always tries to be fair to both sides.

She would call me and check up on me, ask me what was going on and what my plans were. If she saw I was lost somehow, she would give me examples of people she knew that went through the same. She would tell me words of her pastor in the Sunday service, and I always ended up empowered and with hope in my heart. According to Dr Wayne Dyer, when you pray you are talking to God. And when your intuition talks, it's God talking to you! In this case, I often felt that God was talking to me through her. Sometimes she would call me and tell me exactly what I needed to hear. Other days when my faith was down, she would strengthen it by saying: 'I know you will do great. There are no second options because God is leading your way. Put it in His hands, worship Him and you will see in yourself what me and Him already did. Trust Him and wait everything will come to you at the right time.'

Tuxa, your words of wisdom during my difficult times were the best present you ever gave me. You were my bridge with God when my faith was weak. I am forever grateful. May God always bless and protect your family.

*'If you treat me like an option, then I'll leave you like a choice'.*
*– Divyanjali Verma –*

# In the end, I found peace instead of tears

2014 was finally here, and Pedro was scheduled to travel in the middle of the month of January. In the weeks before he went, he told me to apply for benefits, as he had to put his job on hold at the hotel with no payment. Right there it showed me that he had already made his mind up. We had £200 in savings and £50 in my account, and he took his last salary with him. According to him, I was now a single mother, and certainly they would give me Income Support and Jobseeker's Allowance (laugh). I just heard what he had to say and applied for the benefits. I remember crying on the phone to the lady because she asked me so many questions and I started to feel overwhelmed. I felt like a low-life woman that couldn't even provide for her child. At the same time, I had my uni exams coming up, and I didn't want to allow stress to win me over. I had come a long way with my studies; I was aiming for a first-class honours degree and I wouldn't let anyone get in the way of it. I remember one day I was studying, and Pedro came into the room to ask me: 'So, are you prepared to stay alone with Gabriel?'

All I said was: 'I have an exam coming up! Do you mind?' What the hell – is this man for real? I couldn't wait for him to go anymore; his presence was now irritating me.

The night before his flight to Angola, he tried to have sex with me, and I told him not to touch me. He woke up in the morning, got ready, and before he left, he came to kiss me and said: 'I love you very much!' I didn't respond and went straight back to sleep again. After a few hours, Gabriel woke me up, and I was in such a good mood. We went downstairs, I had breakfast with my son and then decided to deep clean the house. I took all of his pictures down, took all of his clothes and shoes out of my room, put them in black bags and out of my way. I put on loud music while doing all of this and danced and laughed with my son in between all the things I was doing. That was a good day, and I was determined to have a good day before the storm. He went on a Saturday, and my exam was on the Monday. I went and I did it with confidence: I'd studied for it, was ready and knew I was going to pass.

Before Pedro went, I had already gone to an interview at Attraction World (a tourism company that sells trips to attractions). Kathryn, my year manager, put me forward for it. She said: 'Aurea, it's perfect for you. They are asking us to send our best students, so I thought of you!' The interview went well, but they said they would let me know by the end of the month. After my exam, my days were pretty much taken up by applying for jobs, going to the council to resolve paperwork and applying for things to get money. Everything was like reading Chinese to me, as Pedro was in control of those kind of things before. Some days I would be up and hopeful, looking for jobs, and others I would be down and depressed in bed all day while Gabriel was in nursery doing the free hours he was entitled to.

I remember one day Elisabete called me to ask how I was, how I felt, or I was supposed to feel. I was feeling low, not because Pedro left, but because I had nothing productive to do. My life was reduced to being a mother and worrying about where the money would come from to pay bills, eat, and keep the roof above our heads. She told me everything was going to be fine and, if I needed money, to let her know. I told her not to worry, that God never failed me, and eventually he was going to give me what was fit for me – a job or benefits! The next day, I received an email from my soon-to-be-manager Gordon, saying that Attraction World would be happy to have me, and to let him know when I was available to start. 'God is good all the time!'

I had almost two weeks to organise myself with childcare. I talked to my friend Dalila about it and she offered to take and pick-up Gabriel from nursery for me, as his nursery was on the way to her work. I spoke to the nursery regarding Gabriel going full-time and took care of everything I needed to. I was now a new graduate from UCB with a 2:1 hons in BA Tourism Business Management and starting my first proper job in the UK in the area I'd studied for. In the midst of what was going on in my life, I had something to feel happy and proud about: I DID IT!

I didn't tell Pedro I got a job or respond to any of his text messages/phone calls after he got to Angola. After a week of being there, he called to say that he got a job with his friend and had decided to stay. I thought: 'Boy, please, you think I am stupid? You decided that ages ago and you probably had the job offer before you left UK.'

I just said: 'Good for you,' and switched off the phone.

After that, he would call home and I would tell Gabriel to answer the phone. I was annoyed with him and for everything that came after he left. When I started applying for single mother benefits, they started asking questions about my previous circumstances, and I responded to the best of my knowledge and truthfully. Not long after, I started receiving letters with fines, others to pay money back for misleading information. I was livid with him, but it was also my fault for being so stupid and naïve as to let a man take control like that.

I told Dalila about it, and she told me to go to the council and revenue and give all Pedro's personal details of where he was, so they could send half the bills to him, and that's exactly what I did. As I was always honest with the revenue and council people, and they could see I was lost in most issues, they were always very helpful and understanding with me. I remember the lady in the council saying to me once to make sure I asked him to take his name off the house documents, otherwise, he could go back and claim rights to it. So, I did, but it took him three years to finally decide to sign the papers the council and I sent to him. The council had to pressure him to do so by saying that, if he still wanted his name on the house, he needed to pay half the rent, because I was refusing to do so. For two years, my life was work and paying present and past bills like rent, council tax and revenue money that was previously overpaid to us because of his declarations. I was always at zero, and sometimes I had to use my credit card to buy food or other necessary things, and that's how I got myself in more debt. But, as hard as it felt, I always tried to see things in a positive way: the bills were being paid, I had my job and me and my son were healthy. I felt happy and blessed.

After five months, Pedro came back on holiday for two weeks! I didn't let him stay at the house, so he had to go to his brothers. I had too much resentment and anger toward him at the time to allow him to stay under the same roof with me. Every time we would talk, it ended up in an argument. Eventually, we talked about our differences and he asked me, if he decided to stay, could we work things out. I told him I wasn't sure, that it would take time to trust him again and I didn't want him in the house until we worked out our issues completely. We had sex a few times and I knew that, in his mind, all was resolved, that he just needed to give me more time to 'cool down' (laugh). He started giving the impression to people that we were together again. I was just enjoying the performance of someone that always took me for a fool and for granted.

A few days before he was leaving, he came to talk to me. He said he knew we still loved each other, and we should stick to our love. I should be patient, he said, and give him at least five years in Angola so he could make the money he needed and then come back here to open a business. I said: 'You know my family story (apart from the HIV – Pedro wouldn't know how to deal with it, as he is very ignorant with certain things), you know that my parents had a life of a long-distance relationship, you know what that did to my family, you know how much I hated it. So, what makes you think that I would want that for myself?

He said: 'But my future is there!'

And I said: 'That's the thing! You, yourself and you, again! What about me, what about Gabriel, what about your other children? You only think about yourself! I am thinking about me and Gabriel and what's best for him and for us. I am not leaving my house, my job and giving up a comfortable life to go live in your auntie's house in an unstable country. So, as I told you before, you need to decide what is best for you and your family, because I've already made my decision.'

He looked at me and said: 'I am sorry that you feel that way. I am at a time of my life that financial stability is more important than family. I am going; I need to go!'

I smiled and said: 'I am sorry that you feel that way too. I hope you never regret those words! In that case, we are definitely done. Please take all your stuff, otherwise I will give it to charity.' He tried to keep talking, but I left the house and went for a drive with Gabriel, to give him space to clear everything and get out of my way.

It took me five years to come to terms with the way things finished between Pedro and me. I couldn't care less about him. I didn't have any more feelings for him. Even when we had sex, it was because it was easier to have it with him than go look for someone new: it was familiar and effortless. I didn't have the energy or the time to put into new men or to go on dates; my mind wasn't even in that space at that time. Also, contradictory to what men think, women have needs too, so when he was there and available: 'Why Not?'

My problem with Pedro was and will always be Gabriel. What he said offended me for my son, it was out of order. I didn't consider myself his family anymore, but Gabriel is for the rest of his life. How can you say that money is more important than your children? For real? Also, he focused so much on the money factor, however, since he'd been in Angola, we'd had constant arguments because he didn't pay child support. At the beginning he would try to send it every six months. Then he just stopped doing so. When I asked for it, he would say that I needed to understand it was difficult to take money out of Angola because of all the bureaucracy. I don't have to understand anything: you made your choice, now deal with that and grow up. You should be the one understanding that a child has to eat and be dressed, that having children is a responsibility. If you are not there to help with childcare, then at least help financially. He never had money to send to his children, but people would tell me about  his  party posts on Facebook or whatever. Our arguments were always over this. I would say to him: 'If you are not paying, then I won't let you see or talk to Gabriel.'

## You are what you are

However, with time, I came to understand I was damaging my son. He missed his dad; he didn't understand money matters; all he wanted was his dad and he shouldn't pay for Pedro's lack of responsibility or my rage against him. So, I started to breathe more regarding this subject and learn to cool down. I can't control what I can't control, so let me control what I can. Also, I was fortunate enough to have a job that allowed me, in those five years, to grow, and it paid me enough to have a comfortable life with my son. So, I decided I was done arguing with Pedro over money; if he didn't know his obligations, I wasn't willing to school him anymore, as that was a painful and exhausting process.

In August 2019, Pedro paid for Gabriel to go to Portugal to stay with him for five weeks. This came after two years without seeing Gabriel and no financial help (but they would talk over WhatsApp). When he came to take Gabriel, I invited him to come and have lunch one of the days, as we needed to talk. Also, Gabriel wanted to show him his new room and the decoration he'd chose for it. The day he came, I could see the happiness in my child's face. Gosh, I feel like crying just thinking about it. We ate, we laughed, we talked about everything and everyone (family wise), we had a good time, and my son was over the moon.

After I cleaned the kitchen, I said to Pedro we should talk 'business', and I started: 'I don't know if you noticed, but I am done fighting with you over your obligations. From now on, I will abstain from comments regarding your daddy duties; but I will not hide them from Gabriel when you fail to do so. If you are supposed to do something but you don't and it affects him, I will tell him the truth. Not in a spiteful way, but I will tell him the truth if it needs to be told. If he doesn't know why you acted a certain way, I will tell Gabriel to call you and ask you. And I would appreciate you telling him the truth. Gabriel is very intelligent for an eight-year-old. He is very perceptive but also very sensitive. He, just like me, hates it when people hide or lie, so from now on there will be transparency. I will be accountable for my things and you for yours. I am done being the bad guy because of your lack of consistency. I am done lying and disappointing Gabriel for you. You are his dad: act like one and be accountable for your mistakes.

Gabriel is living in a fantasy world where he thinks that everything great in his life comes from you, and everything bad comes from me, because I am the one disciplining him, educating him, teaching him routine, etc. I already do enough; I can't be you as well! Also, I understand that you can't help monthly with child costs, but if you could guarantee me that during all the big school holidays you will have him to stay, I will be your best friend. You know childcare is expensive in this country, and what you did this summer helped me a lot and Gabriel also benefited from it. He became more confident and happier; that's all I want for my child.

I don't want you to promise me anything but would like you to consider and think about it. Please note that this is the last time I will have this sort of conversation with you. I just wanted to let you know that the Wanuza that you left five years ago has died. This Wanuza now aims for excellence for herself and for her child. If becoming your friend to the best of my abilities makes my son happy, then that's what I am going to do from now on. When you are around, I will be polite to you and even do things with the three of us if Gabriel asks us to.

You are free to see it the way you feel entitled to (because he is the type of man that, if I am being nice to him, automatically thinks I want him back); your judgement doesn't bother me anymore. I am coming to you like a blank page trying to co-exist and co-parent with you. Gabriel is my responsibility as much as he is yours.'

He looked at me, surprised, and said: 'I appreciate that.'

Then he was going to make excuses again about money, and I told him: 'I am not interested; those are your circumstances and your problems. I don't need to know what is going on in your life, just honour your obligations. How you do it or what you do to make it happen is not my problem. I do the same every day since you left!'

Then I looked at Gabriel and asked: 'Are you happy that we are all here and Mommy and Daddy are being good to each other?'

And he said: 'Yes Mommy. I just want you to be friends and talk without shouting!'

That day, I drew a line in the sand for the sake of mine and my son's sanity. Those five years, I was so focused on being right that I didn't see how much that was affecting my son. I didn't love Pedro anymore, but I did resent him leaving me with a child, with no money in a country where I didn't have any family around to help. The fact I struggled financially sometimes, and he didn't help, would leave me livid and in rage with him to a point where, sometimes, I would call him and shout down the phone while Gabriel was around. I am ashamed of all those moments: I thought I was fighting a battle for my son, fighting for his rights, and although it is true, I was using my personal pain in the process, so the communication was not clear. Also, it is difficult to make a man understand his parental responsibilities when he believes in his own excuses. It's like talking to a wall. I can't understand his way of moving in life. I tried but it seems so low, so greedy, so unhumble, so lost and out of purpose that I stopped trying to understand. Until he puts his children first in his life and realises how much he is missing, I have nothing else to say to him as, from where I am sitting, he is a lost cause!

# To Pedro: I can't teach you how to be a father... still, your son loves you like one

Pedro, I don't have much to forgive you for. I thought I did, that I should forgive you for being irresponsible with your obligations to our son, but I think that is something that perhaps is between you and Gabriel. One day he will grow up and understand or know the contribution his dad had, or otherwise, in his life. It annoys me that you don't fulfil your obligations, but you do what you want to do. You have always been like that (selfish) and I don't think you will change any time soon. I forgive you for leaving me with a child and no money, for deciding to go live your life and leave us without a financial plan, given that you were the one working. I hold a grudge against you regarding that part, but I think it is time to let that feeling go. I wish I could do the same with you, but unfortunately, until Gabriel is old enough, we still have to deal with each other (sigh).

You think that I hate you because you left us. I don't! The way I see it, I left you first, as I had decided to not continue with our relationship anymore. My anger towards you was always for the way you left me hanging with bills and no money and a child to raise on my own, for what you said and how offensive that was to my son. I want you to know that I wish for you to get rich in Angola (since the money is there) and to do well in life. You are my son's father and wishing you bad things is the same as wishing them on my son. I love him too much to allow rage to take control of me in that sense. I am sorry I put too many expectations on you over the years. I thought that education would be the way for you to stop being such a caveman and more of a progressive thinker, but I came to the conclusion that some people can study all their lives but, if they are stuck in unhealthy cultural cycles, they can be just as ignorant when they are an educated person. I always knew you were not the man for me, but let myself believe that, if we worked hard enough, we would be fine. Today I see that our paths needed to cross, that Gabriel needed to be here, but we do not need to be together for him to exist and evolve as a human being.

Finally, I have nothing much to forgive you for, but I have a lot to thank you for. You deciding to stay in Angola set me free to live my life the way God intended me to. Perhaps, if you had not gone, we would still be trying for Gabriel, for our families, or for your other children. I don't know about you, but I am happy with my life right now. I have matured and grown as a woman. I now know who I am, and I am not allowing any man to come into my life anymore and take control over it, making me financially and emotionally dependent. I have nothing but love for you, not just because we have a beautiful son together, but because there was a time when we were good friends and you helped me at a time when I had no one else to turn to. Thank you for that and for the life lessons you taught me. Thank you for our son; he is the best present you ever gave me. May we continue to be the best parents we can be for Gabriel. He didn't ask to come into this world, so we definitely owe him that.

*'The problem is not the problem. The problem is your attitude about the problem.'*
 *– Ann Brashares –*

# Chapter 4
# Patrick – 'The Monster behind the gentleman'

*Beware of destination addiction: The idea that happiness is in the next place, the next job, or even with the next partner. Until you give up the idea that happiness is somewhere else, it will never be where you are.*
- *Robert Holden* –

After two years alone, I felt it was time to give love a shot. Gabriel was five-and-a-half and, being a boy, I thought he needed a man's influence in his life. I remember talking about that with friends of mine, and they used to make fun of me (in the good sense) by saying: 'Where are you going to find a man? In the supermarket? You don't like to go out; your life is work, home and Gabriel. You have a routine in place, and you don't seem to want to make space for anything else. Where is the man going to fit in?'

That was very true: it is too much effort to have a man, to look for romance, or go on dates. I did have a few sexual encounters with men I met on the few times I went out. One was through work, and another one when out with my friends Catarina and Raimonda. But, like I said, it was just fun, nothing special, nothing to wonder about and no one to actually have a relationship with. But I thought it was time to settle down, felt I was ready for it and I started talking to people about it and listening to their advice.

One day at work, my manager Annette asked me about my love life. I told her it was pretty much non-existent, but I was looking forward to changing that asap. She asked me if I'd ever considered online dating, and I told her I found it a bit dodgy. She told me that, given my circumstances, maybe it was the best option, because I could control when, how and ensure suitability. I always respect Annette's opinion, as she is always so accurate and doesn't say anything without knowledge on the subject. I went home, did my research and, voila, I created a page at Match.com. I must say that my first few days on the web were very depressing; the amount of people I talked to, the crap I heard, was unbelievable.

The second week, I narrowed my choices, and ended up finding a gentleman that interested me very much. His name was Patrick, and he was black, of Caribbean descent, a businessman, well spoken, forty nine years old, intellectual, a father-of-two and living in Birmingham. It sounded like his profile was done with me in mind. From the day I started talking with him, it was amazing how the conversation flowed so nicely. We would talk about everything for hours, with long texts back and forth, clear communication, an amazing connection and mutual interests. Rob, one of my teachers in uni, once called me a progressive thinker. At the time, I didn't know what that meant, but then I understood I loved a person that could challenge and motivate me intellectually. I guess one of the reasons I fell out of love with Pedro is because I got bored of the sameness of our life, of his cultural prison cycle of old beliefs and lack of communication. Patrick was the opposite, and that was what captivated me in the first place. We exchanged numbers so the communication would be easier between us but, after two days of good communication, he disappeared from the website and stopped responding to my texts.

I was a bit disappointed but didn't think much of it and continued on with my life. By the middle of the following week, he texted me again saying: 'Hi Aurea, sorry I went silent, but if you are still free, perhaps we could have a coffee and a chat in person?'

I asked him: 'What happened to you? You disappeared!' He said he was dating this lady, and since they were going on a third date, he thought it was only right to come off the website and give it a try, but it turned out the woman was crazy, and he was not up to craziness at that time of his life. I told him I understood perfectly well, and we could meet on Saturday of that week. I told him I was meeting my friends for an afternoon tea at the Hyatt Hotel in Birmingham, and we could meet there after that. On the day, I made sure I told him to come at a time I knew my friends were still going to be there: I wanted to make sure they were going to see his face and, before I gave them a signal that everything was all right, they could not leave for any reason.

On the day, he called me again and I thought he wanted to bail out, but he said he just wanted to have a pre-date conversation and see if it was worth us spending time on the date. We talked for an hour, and he told me he hadn't had a proper relationship in nine years, that he had a degree in psychology but never practised it as he always worked and continued to work as a recruitment agent, but now he owned his own company. We both laughed; the conversation was easy, enjoyable and interesting. That left both of us wanting more, so we stuck to our previous plan.

He arrived looking glamorous, well groomed, and charming. I looked at him and felt instantly nervous.

He looked at me and said: 'Gosh, you look really young!'

I said: 'Don't worry. I am thirty-five years old for sure; I can show you my ID.'

That was the icebreaker. Then I said: 'You look like Idris Elba.'

'Yes, I know; I get that a lot!'

We talked for a while at the bar and then we decided to sit at a table. When the waitress came to give us our drinks, he kept looking at her ass and boobs. So, I stopped talking and asked him: 'Are you enjoying the view?'

He said: 'I am sorry. I must tell you I do have a problem with that, and I am working very hard in therapy to overcome that. But at the same time, why would women dress like that if they don't want men to look?'

I said: 'Wow, you do have a long way to go in therapy if that is the way you think!' and he started laughing. What he said, put me off. Looking back, that was my first red flag, and I should have just picked my things up and left. But we stayed there we talked for an hour or so and then decided to go to the cinema. Before that he asked me if we could go and drop his shopping bags at his apartment, as he lived around there. On the way to his house, he started telling me how much he spent on clothes, which brands, and how important it is to dress well.

That put me off again, and I thought: 'Well, me and you will never work out, because I love my Primark and I am a tomboy!' Then I thought the only reason he came with his shopping bags to the date and asked me to go with him to drop them at home was to impress me, so I could see where he lived and shopped at.

I am not a materialistic girl, so things like that don't impress me. Like any other woman, I love beautiful and nice things, but I can still get them cheaper from Primark. I refuse to bankrupt myself like some people do just to have the latest fashion. For me, it is all about personal taste. If you have good taste and a sense of fashion, you dress well in any brand. If you don't, you can be wearing Louis Vuitton and look ridiculous. I said that to him, and his response was: 'Don't be ridiculous! If you are to be dating me, Primark is for sure not on the list!'

I responded: 'If it's me buying, trust me, Primark will be on the top of the list!'

He laughed and said I had a bit of attitude, which was typical in black women. But he thought that, because I'm light skinned, I would probably be more whitish than blackish! My black attitude came out for real, and I said: 'What kind of crap are you trying to say? Whatever it is, I don't appreciate it!'

He laughed and said: 'Calm down! It came out wrong, but it was a compliment! I've had my share of white women but now I am looking for a sister, but the attitude black women have puts me off. Black women don't listen and have problems obeying.'

I said: 'How old are you again? You sound worse than my grandfather.' (Not that I have ever met any of mine).

He laughed again and said: 'Oh, I see. You are one of those with a smart mouth?'

I didn't respond, just gave him a side-look and asked if we were still going to the cinema. I thought to myself: 'We can go to the cinema but, after that, I am not going to entertain this. No wonder he has been alone for nine years.'

He saw me shift as I became quieter and let him do the talking. I wasn't impressed at all anymore (I can't stand arrogant and chauvinistic men). As it was still early for our movie, we went to the bar in front of the cinema. He asked for whiskey and I asked for a coke. He looked at me and said: 'Come on, have something else. A cocktail maybe?'

'No thanks. I already had wine at the hotel, plus I am not much of a drinker, so will fall asleep in the movie, and I am also driving.'

'Fair enough! A strong-minded woman you are, Aurea. I like and admire it in a woman.'

I just smiled and didn't say anything back. However, after that his arrogant attitude changed, he became softer and chivalrous. We kept talking and found out we loved the same movies old and new. In that moment, it was like we started the night all over again. I started liking him then, and it came to a point where I thought: 'He is not that bad. A bit of a jerk sometimes, but not bad at all.'

Our movie session finished around 1 a.m. When we came out of the cinema, it was snowing with the first snow of the year. I took him home as it was on my way. When we got to his house, he asked me if I wanted to come up for a drink. I said it was a bit late and was not sure it was a good idea. He said: 'Don't worry, I won't touch you, and I can leave the door wide open, so if you scream the security guard can hear you.'

I laughed and said: 'All right; I will come for tea!'

He shared his house with a friend. He told me the friend moved in with him after divorcing and, most weekends, he would go back to his hometown to see his kids. We talked more, watched another movie (barely) and then I decided to go. When he opened the door of his house, it was snowing heavily, and I remember thinking: 'Oh shit, how am I going to get home tonight?!'

He straight away said: 'I don't feel great letting you leave in this snow! It's not safe; you should stay.'

I felt uneasy for a bit, but I was thinking the same. I hate driving in heavy rain or snow. I was quiet and thinking about which was safer; to go home in that snow or spend the night in the house of a total stranger!

Then he said: 'Listen, text your mom or whoever you want with my full name and address. I can also give you the reception number so they can call the security guard or come here if they don't hear from you by tomorrow morning.'

I thought that was fair enough, so we went back in. I texted my mother saying I was going to stay in Birmingham for the night because of the snow, then texted my friend Tuxa and told her everything and gave her all details that she needed, just in case, and told her I would text her before noon. If not, at least she knew what to do.

After that, he gave me his tracksuit, a t-shirt and socks to wear. I went to change in the bathroom, and I remember feeling so out of place: this wasn't in the plan. I am the one that always plays safe, the one that doesn't like one-night stands, and this was taking me out of my comfort zone.

However, he was being a gentleman all the way, so I was trying to just breathe and relax. I came out of the bathroom and he was putting on another movie for us to watch. He asked me if I was comfy and if I wanted another cup of tea. I remember following him to the kitchen to make sure he didn't put anything dodgy in my drink. We then went back to his room to watch something else; I don't even remember what. I was so tired, but all I could think was 'what would my mother think if she knew I was in a situation like this!' She didn't even know I was on a date; I told her I was meeting my friends and that was it. I felt so irresponsible putting myself in a situation like that.

I guess Patrick felt I was tense. He held my hand and said: 'Relax. I'm not going to hurt you or force myself onto you. Let's just chill. You can lay down if you want; I can see that you are tired.'

I said thank you, but I was OK for now. We continued to talk, and, after a while, he said: 'Can I kiss you?'

I looked at him surprised and not knowing what to say. No one ever asked me that; normally a man will just kiss me if they see I am open to it. I didn't reply, but I leant over to kiss him. It wasn't spectacular, didn't give me butterflies in my stomach. To be honest, it wasn't a great kiss: it was 'dry' and unromantic but made me feel relaxed and gave me a sense that I could trust him. We cuddled after that and he said: 'This is what I miss the most: the cuddles and the intimacy. For me, that is more important in a relationship than sex!'

I agree with him, and for me that moment was perfect, and the moment I let go of all my guards and let Patrick in without a second thought. We didn't have sex, but it was the best first night I ever spent with a man. I didn't feel pressured to do anything, and I could see that all he wanted was to just lay down close to me and hold me tight.

The next day he woke up and went to the shop to buy things for breakfast. While we were preparing the breakfast, I noticed he was talking about us like we were an item already, so I said: 'The way you are talking almost seems like we are a couple already?'

He responded: 'Yes, I do feel good about the idea, and I do think it could work. What about you?'

I said: 'I liked it too, but we went out one night; maybe we should give it a couple of days before making decisions on the spur of the moment and then regretting it.'

'I am a grown-up man; I know what I want. I chose you to be with me. You have got my attention now and I want to explore it. In fact, just to show you my commitment, I will come off the website, so you know that I am not playing around.'

My head was as big as it could be, instead of analysing his words: 'I chose you,' and 'you got my attention.' I felt special and desired! This intelligent and put-together man went on one date with me and now he was deciding to devote his sole attention to me. I smiled at him and said: 'In that case, I will do the same!'

Over the next three days, things between us went into speed mode. I remember him introducing me to his flat mate on one of the days and him saying we had a good connection going on and that it almost seemed like we had been together for ages.

After a few days, I received a notification from my manager at work asking me if I wanted/could go to Orlando, as one of my colleagues on the list couldn't go. Of course, I said yes: everyone at the company always wants to go on the industry trips to Orlando!

I called Patrick straight away to give him the news. He wasn't very pleased at the beginning, because we already had plans for the weekend. But then he said: 'Perhaps before you go, you can spend some time with me?'

I agreed. That night, I went to meet him at his office to have dinner with him. He took his time to ask me more personal questions, but his focus was around who I dated or saw after Pedro and if it was serious. I told him that I didn't have time or the focus for a serious relationship after my separation, but I did have an affair with a married man I knew through work for a couple of weeks, and a recent fling with a twenty-five-year-old I met on a night out the summer before I met him. Straight away, he started being judgmental and asking me the reasons why I would choose to have such low-life romantic experiences. I did try to explain to him that, where I was emotionally at that time of my life, those choices made me feel good about myself, made me feel alive, desired and beautiful. But I always knew it was nothing that would last and, looking back, I feel pathetic that I let my low self-esteem get the best of me (regarding the married man). Eventually, we moved away from this subject but, right there, I found out Patrick was very judgmental. He would say: 'I am a truthful person. I like honesty. I don't like surprises in my relationships of any kind, and when I ask questions it's because I am trying to understand the person I have in front of me!'

I then took the opportunity to ask him about himself. He told me he had three therapists, and I found it odd and worrying. He saw that in my face and tried to explain to me the different approaches each one of them had in different sections of his life. The main problematic areas were his relationship with his mother and grandmother – he hated them to his core – and the relationship with his daughters, which was non-existent with the younger one, and a work in progress with the oldest.

That night, I got a bit worried about what he told me regarding his relationship with his mother and grandmother. One thing I know is that a man that doesn't respect his own mother will not respect you. So, I was worried about that, and eventually I was proven to be right. Also, what I found out with time was that he demanded honesty, but he couldn't handle the truth: whatever 'secrets' or truths about myself I would choose to share with him, he would use as a weapon to hurt me.

## One Silly Mistake, showed me who you are

My trip to Orlando was great, as I went with a nice group of colleagues. As soon I got there, I gave all the hotel's contact details to Patrick so he could call me. He told me it would be easier to call me at the hotel than to use WhatsApp, because of the connection. Regardless of the time zone, we would talk for hours at night and in the morning. I would be so exhausted. One of the nights after a cocktail party, we got to the hotel around 1 a.m. I texted him when I got in, as he asked me to do, so he knew I was all right. I was a bit tipsy and, stupidly, I decided to see if I could make him jealous, just to check how much he liked me. I sent him a text saying the guy I had an affair with was also there, and he was at the dinner and kept buying me drinks (again, stupid idea). OMG: first I had a long message saying how disrespectful that was towards him and he wasn't staying with someone that was owned by someone else.

I was then trying to reply to his message, and he called my room at 2 a.m. My colleague was already asleep, so I had to jump out of my bed so the noise wouldn't wake her up. As soon as I answered the phone, the man didn't let me talk. I tried to say to him that I was joking, but it came to a point that he was so agitated, upset and shouting that I thought: 'If I tell him I was just joking, it will be even worse.' So, I just let him talk and talk and talk; I'd never felt so much rage in one person's voice. I felt so bad that I had upset him so much that all I could do was apologise and cry. In the end, he asked me how much longer that person was going to stay there for, and I lied, saying he was going the next day. He then said we would have this conversation again when I arrived in the UK and, for now, I should just enjoy the rest of my trip.

I went to bed, and my colleague who heard all the conversation said: 'Aurea, didn't you just start with this guy? How come he is already making you cry and be shaken up like that?' I told her it was my fault, and I explained to her exactly what happened, and she said: 'Even though that is true, he had no right to talk to you the way he spoke and to call you at this time of the night to leave you in that distress. Look at the state you are in: you weren't even able to tell him it was a stupid joke? And when you told him that you were tipsy, he should've just said we can talk tomorrow or when you are back. He seems toxic to me. As your friend, I urge you to be careful. Trust me, been there, done that!'

I didn't pay much attention to what she said. All I could think was that I was so stupid to upset that amazing man that had fallen into my life, and I couldn't lose him over my childish and stupid mistake. Cindy (my colleague) was wrong: he wasn't toxic, he was just upset because I made him angry and he was right to be.

I couldn't make myself enjoy the rest of my trip; my head was on Patrick most of the time. I think I thought more about him than I thought about my son. I was in an internal conflict. One minute I would think to myself: Whatever: if he doesn't want me when I go back, there are plenty of fish in the sea, I've only been seeing him for a couple of days anyway .... The next minute I would think about how difficult it was to find someone that accepts you as a package (with a son), wants to take care of you and your child and is a gentleman. In my head I thought I had found the perfect man for me and a good role model for Gabriel. All of a sudden, I would go back to a place of despair, and my neediness for that man. I could not let him go without a fight or begging for a second opportunity.

When I arrived back, I went to see him straight away. He received me better than I had expected. I waited until he finished work so we could talk. When the time came, I started seeing a different person in him, but I was so blinded by my guilt that I kept making excuses for his behaviour. We went for dinner, and he started by saying that he didn't share and that whatever was still going on between me and my married friend needed to be sorted far from him.

I tried to tell him exactly what happened, that it was a bad joke, but his words were: 'See! People like you are like that: when you are caught, you always try to deny, lie or make the other person feel bad about the dramas that you create. You are just like my mother! Always with men hiding in the corner and every now and then bringing them out according to her needs.'

I sat there looking at him talking about his mother and all of a sudden I said: 'I am sorry you feel that way about your mother, but I am not her. I am sorry about the mess I created, but I already apologised. I don't know what else you want me to do. It almost seemed like I killed someone. JESUS.'

He looked at me and said: 'I feel very uneasy about this relationship, and perhaps we should take things slowly. And, so you know, I am back on the dating website.'

'So, what does that mean to me for us?' I asked.

'It means that I don't mind being your friend. We can keep doing things together, but not romantically. You have loads of issues; you are like a train wreck and if I am not careful you are going to destroy my life. You have loose ends, all over: your mother, Pedro, your ex from your job. And you carry them around like it's normal. A mature and healthy person would have got rid of them already before getting into a relationship with a person like me. I am an alpha male and I need an alpha female with me. You want something that you can't have or are not prepared to have. Being with a person like me requires work and you are not on that level. You don't have the knowledge and teaching you would require time and patience that I don't have. I am too old to even be dealing with a person like you.'

'Wow, you've made me feel just like my mother does at times! I am never good enough for anything. What do you want me to do? Throw my mother out of my house, stop talking with Pedro and leave my job to please you? You are talking about people that have done nothing to cause any harm to our relationship, so I don't get why are you bringing them into this conversation?'

He started raising his voice and using a tone that I didn't appreciate: 'The fact that you don't understand just proves that you are not ready to co-exist without drama. I have a problem with these people because they own you: they live in your head and they manage you. If I was to be with you, I would never be able to penetrate your brain and bring you sense, because they control every aspect of your life.'

I said: 'Most definitely not! I have a history with my mom of love and hate but, in the end, I always end up doing what suits me. I used to seek her approval, but not anymore. Regarding Pedro: he is the father of my child. I don't have to love him, but I respect him in the best way I can for the sake of my son. And about my colleague: until when will you continue to throw that in my face? Almost makes me feel like I can't tell you anything. Is that what you do? Find people's secrets and continuously remind them of their mistakes? GOSH.'

He looked at me, gave me a cynical smile and said: 'I just realised that you are a narcissistic bitch!' He paid the bill and told me: 'Let's go.'

I was silent but having a conversation with myself in my head: Narcissistic! Me? I'd heard that word before, but the idea I had associated with it was pretty much close to a psychopath. I was so focused on that word that I didn't pay attention to the fact he also called me bitch. No one ever called me a bitch (not to my face). I actually googled the word narcissistic on the way home, while in the taxi.

**Narcissistic:** 'having or showing an excessive interest in or admiration of oneself and one's physical appearance'

I was confused: if that was the real meaning, he was more of a narcissist than me! I just continued being silent until we got to his house. He continued giving me the silent treatment, being agitated around the place and his face was completely different, like he was on an internal rage and deciding what to do or say next. I was having none of that. I was tired and wanted to go home to my son now. I'd had enough of long and heavy conversations for the night. With Patrick, every conversation was heavy, emotionally excruciating, and exhausting. Ninety-five per cent of the time I had to just agree with him or go silent so we could move on from the topic, shut him up, or just be able to sleep peacefully without him waking me up in the middle of the night because he wanted to continue to make me understand why he was right. I picked up all of my things that were in his room, then went to find him in the living room and asked him if he could call me an Uber to take me home. He looked at me with his rageful face and said: 'Thought you were staying for the night!'

I told him I was, but now I felt the need to go home. He asked me if I could wait until he finished smoking, so I did. When he came to find me in the room, he was a different person again: soft, sweet, and talkative. 'I saved a few movies to watch with you. Let me show you! Do you want to go get yourself comfortable and pour us some wine?'

I was confused again. What the hell? Did he just forget that I told him I wanted to go home? So, I said: 'Patrick, I was going home!'

'Ah, it's late, and if it's because of your little man, I am sure he is already in bed, so you can go in the morning. Let's just chill and rest for tonight.'

I didn't see any harm in that, so I stayed, and the rest of the evening was good.

That same week, he ended it with me over the phone. I tried to talk him out of it by trying to make him see I liked him very much and was willing to do whatever work he wanted me to do. But he said it was for the best, so *I was* left sad but not broken. I went to pick up the rest of my things the next day and tried to act as put together as I could. I talked to him without giving too much away and he even said he was impressed at how good I looked and sounded. After two days, he called me and said he'd made a mistake. Could I go to see him, as he wanted to talk? I was super happy but didn't give much away as I didn't want to create expectations then get there and take a cold shower. (Be disappointed)

Basically, if I knew then what I know today, I should have taken that first break-up and run for my life. This man that seemed to be so charming, so put-together, the best man that ever appeared in my life, turned out to be a Grandiose Narcissist. The unfolding of his character was done layer by layer by my therapist, Ian. But I've only understood the definition of narcissistic 100 per cent recently, while watching the programme *Red Table Talk* with Jada Pinkett Smith.

## You tried to break me with your twisted ways

Our break-up was around the time my mother left, and Pedro came to the UK to visit Gabriel; I was vulnerable and upset with the way things were left between me and my mother, but happy that she was gone for now because I needed space from her. Patrick was also super-happy about it: in his own words, the only reason he also decided to give us a shot was because my mother was gone. It was always strange to me why he disliked her so much. But today I understand that, because he never had a relationship with his mother, he would get annoyed with anyone that had a good relationship with their mother. He even told me once that he didn't understand why Gabriel was so attached to me, since I wasn't a great mother. I had to check him on that by telling him that I was sorry his mother didn't love him but that I did love my son and I didn't appreciate what he'd just said. What he really hated was me defending my mother and Pedro to him, and that's why he would always say that they owned me (lol). Many times, I had to tell him to not talk about them or even my friends that way. I didn't understand that he was a narcissistic but, from an early stage, I saw that he wanted to isolate me from my friends and everything that kept me sane.

But what he didn't understood is that although he probably thought I was weak and needy (which I was, in a way), and he could control me in whatever way he thought. I have been in many dark places in my life. My friends helped me get through most, my mother I knew loved me in her own way and would come to save me from whatever if I needed it, and Pedro gave me a beautiful child and helped me at a crucial time of my life. I was grateful to them, not owned by them. It is difficult to explain that to someone that is loyal/grateful to no one apart from their own ego. I could be disappointed in my mother or Pedro for many reasons, but I know for a fact if I shout 'HELP', they will come for me, and I will never completely close my door to them. I might distance myself from them if they are acting foolishly, and give them space to think about their actions, but they are my and my son's PEOPLE, and no one can delete them from me. Many of our arguments were about it. They were always the times where I, too, would raise my voice and say: 'Don't talk about my mother, Pedro or my friends!'

He would say: 'Are you actually defending these people that have treated you as a utility? And these friends of yours that allowed you to have an affair with a married man and date a twenty-five-year-old and did not try to talk you out of it? Are these the people you are defending? No wonder that your life is a train wreck full of loose ends everywhere!'

He would go on and on for hours, always with the intention of having me back down, apologise and agree with him. The argument would start at 9 p.m. and go until 2 a.m., on a weekday when he knew I had to wake up at 6 a.m. to go to work. Most of it would be monologues because I would not participate. I would not interrupt him during whatever trance he was in, as that would make him even more verbally abusive and agitated, and all I wanted was just for him to stop so I could go to sleep.

I remember the day when we started talking about Pedro for some reason, and arguing in the restaurant around 7 p.m. I was so embarrassed that I couldn't finish my food, and it felt like I had a knot in my throat. I was trying not to cry at the same time, so I just sat there listening to him talking but, as usual, I would just shut down and start singing in my head. That's one of the reasons why I don't remember most of the crap he would say to me. I would go to a safe place in my head where his words wouldn't get to me. He went on and on in the taxi, and still when we got to his house. Eventually he noticed he was talking to himself. That got him even more pissed off, so he started picking on me while I was getting ready for bed, by saying: 'You are a little porky. You need a diet: OMG, look at this (while touching my arms or belly)!'

I would leave the room and go to the bathroom to change there and he would follow me and continue with his abuse:

'Oh, are you trying to hide? No point doing so: everyone can see that you are fat, hiding won't change it!' And then he would start laughing like you only see witches doing in movies. I just kept quiet and went to wash my face as tears started to roll off it.

That night it went on and on. I felt so drained and sick to my stomach, but eventually I fell asleep when he found something else on TV to get him distracted.

In the middle of the night, I woke up feeling sick and a bit dosed up. I picked up my water bottle and ran to the toilet. I vomited and, when I tried to stand up, I felt nausea and passed out. The next minute I woke up with paramedics around me asking me questions and doing all sorts of tests. Nothing came of it; they only said my blood pressure was low and I needed rest. Patrick had his human and pleasant mask on, as he normally did in front of other people. I didn't go to work that day and had to call Dalila to tell her what happened. I stayed with him until the afternoon, but all I wanted was to go home to my surroundings as I was feeling better. Whatever happened that night, I can't explain it, and I don't think I ever will. All I can come up with is that the emotional exhaustion made me feel weak (but I honestly don't know).

After a couple of days, Patrick took that opportunity to start calling me narcissistic and saying I staged everything so I could get his attention, because I was a needy, stupid and self-centred bitch. And I started believing him and doubting myself. He would ask me things and I would just start crying and try to explain, but he would cut me off and start shouting, saying: 'You are a selfish bitch that only thinks about yourself, making me be awake all night because you had to stage feeling sick to get my attention, like being here in my space and my life isn't enough. You are a sad, narcissistic, crazy bitch. You need therapy! You're crazy and you want to destroy me!'

I so believed him that I decided to go to see a therapist! First, I went to see one of the therapists he was seeing, just to know how these things worked. We ended up talking for three hours (he only charged for one though), but he couldn't see me, for obvious reasons, so he gave me the name of colleagues close to my area for me to look up. Patrick offered to pay for it, as he said he wanted to just make sure I would choose a good one and not look at the prices. I chose a Caribbean lady in Walsall, because of a background thing: Black people understand other black people. I saw her twice only, and in those two times she was very specific: 'Sounds to me like you are in a relationship with an abusive and controlling person that is making you doubt yourself.'

I got upset that she said that, and I didn't really connect with her for some reason (maybe because she pointed out the truth and I wasn't ready to receive it). However, I didn't have a chance to continue to see her, as me and Patrick broke up again, and I wasn't expecting him to pay for my therapy then. We broke up because, one weekend, he was going to see his daughter in London. Pedro's mother was in the UK and in London too with her niece. I thought it would be nice to go with Patrick: he could go see his daughter and I would take Gabriel to see his grandmother and dad's family. However, the whole trip started badly. Patrick rented a car (as my car wasn't posh enough for him to go in) and I got to his place late Saturday morning. I left home early, but there was an accident and traffic was bad on the motorway. As soon as I arrived, I saw that the ugly Patrick was present: his eyes were shining in rage and he wanted to go off at me, but he didn't because Gabriel was present. He didn't say a word the entire way to London, apart from asking me to buy food at a petrol station and to tell me that I was late on purpose to make him look bad to his daughter, because I was a selfish bitch. He was saying this in a manner that Gabriel or anyone else couldn't hear him.

For the first time, I told him! 'Don't call me bitch and don't you ever call me any other name again. I haven't given you that right. My parents never called me names and you won't be the first one. Do you understand me?'

I didn't realise I was so loud until he started looking around embarrassed and left to go to the toilet. Damn, that felt so GOOD! I can't even explain.

Back in the car, the mood was back to awkward, but I put music on and was singing to it while Gabriel was playing on the iPad. When we got to London, I left Patrick where he needed to be. As Pedro's cousin (Isaura) stood me up, I went to see my friends Tany, Carla and Carlinha who also lived around there. I stayed with them until late at night, waiting for Patrick to send me the location of the hotel so I could go to meet him. Around midnight, he sent me a text and we headed there. He was still not there, so me and Gabriel got ourselves comfortable and went to sleep. The next morning, he was still in the same mood! I couldn't understand how he went to see his daughter, told me he had a great time, but was still in that ugly and stupid mood. As always, I let him be and then told him that I could only go back to Wolverhampton after 2 p.m., as I'd rearranged with Isaura to see her auntie, because the day before it wasn't possible.

OMG – the house came down. He started getting agitated and I could see the rage in his eyes, but he was controlling himself because of Gabriel. So, he packed all his stuff and said he was leaving by train. I told him to just calm down, that Pedro's cousin would come to the hotel with her auntie, we would sit for a bit, have a drink and then we could head back to the Midlands. He was having none of it, picked up his stuff, gave Gabriel a hug and left. I told Gabriel to wait inside and I followed him to the lift, trying to make him calm down and see some sense. While I was talking, he cut me off and said in the rudest, rageful and domineering manner ever: 'Why are you still talking?'

I had a chill in my spine like I'd never had before in my entire life; I just froze and let him go. It took me a minute to compose myself and get back to the room. I was so disturbed that I too wanted to get home. I called Isaura to ask if she was on the way, but she wasn't picking up. After a few tries I ended up calling one of her daughters, and she told me her mother was sleeping, that they'd been at a party the day before and came home late, so she didn't know what time her mom would be awake.

I felt so stupid. I came all the way from Wolverhampton for Gabriel to spend some time with his dad's family, and none of them bothered to come meet us any of the days. Once again, I felt like Patrick was completely right to be upset with me. If I hadn't decided to come with him to London, he wouldn't have got there late. And If I didn't decide to wait for Pedro's cousin and mother to come and meet us at the hotel on that day, Patrick wouldn't have left as upset as he did. I started packing our things and left the hotel, livid with Isaura. I knew she was very disorganised, but what she did was inconsiderate and disrespectful. I always thought me and his family had a good relationship, but I decided right there it was time to cut the ties. Gabriel was their family, not me; if they weren't bothered to come and see him then I surely shouldn't try either. It's Pedro's family, so he should be the one pushing Gabriel to his side, and I would do the same on my side toward my family.

We got into the car and headed back to Wolverhampton and, as soon as I got on the motorway, Patrick called. As I was driving, I had to put it on loudspeaker. He told me he was back at the hotel as his train was cancelled, but the receptionist had said I was gone already. I told him that, as Pedro's family didn't show up, we ended up leaving sooner. He started shouting on the phone, saying I was like a stupid little girl trying to please everyone except the people that really cared about me, that I'd ruined his weekend, and saying that was my plan all along, that people like me had no consideration for others' time, money and plans. I let him go on for a bit, but then I remembered Gabriel was in the car and I said: 'Do you mind stopping shouting, and being verbally aggressive and abusive? My son is in the car and this is on loudspeaker.'

'Oh, now you care about your son. Did you care about him when you decided to make him travel all the way to London to go see these people that you call his family? People that don't give a shit about him, where he studies, where he lives, what he eats, how he dresses? I do more for him than they ever did, and I am not even his real family.'

I finished the call. He tried to call again, and I didn't pick up. I was in such distressed state, I had to stop at a petrol station to calm myself down, and then I sent him a text saying I would probably get to Birmingham first, so I could pick him up at the train station and take him home to pick up my car from his house. As soon as he got the message, he called again, saying that it was unfortunate he still had to see me again: all he wanted was for me to disappear from his life because he'd had enough of trying to teach me and that I was like a child that doesn't listen and it was exhausting and depressing to be around me. I switched off the phone again, and when I was going to start driving, Gabriel said to me: 'Mom, don't cry; just say sorry to him and he will be OK with you again!'

That made me smile: the innocence of a child is just marvellous. But at same time it made me upset that he humiliated me in front of my son. I felt like he shouldn't do that, and that I sure didn't give him that right (or maybe I did). When I got to Birmingham, I stopped again at a petrol station to see if I had any messages. He'd left one saying what time he was going to arrive and for me to pick him up. When he got to the car, I could still feel the tension, so I started by saying: 'I am sorry about all the mess today, but don't you dare raise your voice or be offensive again in front of my son.'

My voice was firm and angry. His body relaxed a little, he looked at me and said: 'Yes, you are right. Sorry, little man, that you had to listen to me being upset like that. I just want you to know that it has nothing to do with you, alright?'

Gabriel nodded 'OK' and then asked him: 'You are not impressed with my mom today?'

He said nothing more and nothing less than: 'It's adult stuff; don't worry about it!'

I took him home, moved my luggage from the rental car to mine, let him and Gabriel say their goodbyes and then, after Gabriel was in the car, I asked him again: 'Do you want me to disappear?'

'After everything you've done this weekend, what do you think?' he said.

I got home in such a distressed state that Dalila (she was now living with me) didn't know what to do to help me. I asked her to look after Gabriel and I went straight to bed: I was feeling like a lost cause, an incapable person, someone who couldn't do anything right. How could I have lost someone like Patrick? How could I be so stupid? He was right: I am stupid, so stupid …

I cried most of the night! The next day, I called in sick at work as I didn't have enough energy to get out of bed, and my face looked terrible. Dalila checked on me before she left for work and took Gabriel and her daughter to school. I stayed in bed all day, feeling upset with myself and thinking about how I could make things right between me and Patrick, but I never called him.

## Two faces

This went on for two weeks. I continued in my depression, but I tried to keep going as well as possible. I couldn't lose my work too, as I had a child to care for and bills to pay. I ended up taking two weeks as last-minute holidays so I could just be home and do nothing, as I couldn't focus at work.

My first week off work, I decided I needed to make changes in my life. I looked in the mirror and hated what I was seeing. First, I cut my hair and decided to go natural; I always wanted to do that but people in my family would tell me that it wouldn't look great on me because I am light skinned. I just didn't care anymore; I needed a change and a radical one.

Then I went to my GP and told them I wanted to have therapy. The waiting list was gigantic, so I texted Patrick's therapist (the one I'd seen before) and asked if there was any cheaper associate I could go to. He referred me to Cedar

Counselling in Birmingham, and so I started to get the help I needed. I really wanted to do it, but before it was just to impress Patrick.

Then I decided to redecorate my house. Since Pedro had left, everything had been the same. I felt like my house was just a house and not a home. I kept myself busy with things around the house because that was keeping me sane. Although Dalila was living with me, I still felt like I was the only who was bringing income into the house (as she could leave at any time), so I had to put on a face and go to work every day, and I also couldn't rely on her to be taking care of Gabriel all the time, because it wasn't fair on her or Gabriel. Dalila did mention that she was worried, and she felt like me taking two weeks of my holidays to stay home was not a great idea. Perhaps she was right, but I needed to be at home, as I couldn't bear stupid conversations around the office or fake smiles.

Almost at the end of my time off, Patrick sent me a text asking if he could call me. I said yes, so he did. We talked about normal stuff for a while and then, out of the blue, he asked me what I was doing that day. I said not much, and he asked me if I could meet him later and go to therapy with him? I was so happy that he wanted to see me, and I thought the fact he wanted to go to therapy meant he wanted to work things out between us. I told him I had to arrange things with Dalila, but I would get back to him.

That afternoon, I went to meet him at his office, and he wasn't there! As soon as his assistant saw, me became uncomfortable which made me feel suspicious straight away. He had always been so welcoming but this time, I had to push my way into the office. 'Aurea! Is Patrick expecting you?' he asked.

'Yes Michael. Are you OK? You seem nervous.'

He picked up the phone to call Patrick and just said: 'Aurea is here.'

Patrick, straight after, called my phone: 'Hi. You're early!'

I told him I was afraid of getting stuck in traffic, so had decided to come early, but I'd texted him before I left home. Then I asked him if he was going to be long and asked if he wanted me to pick him up wherever he was, but he was very dismissive. I don't know what it is with us women, but I felt straight away that he was with another woman. I could feel it in my stomach, my bones and my heart. I could feel it, smell it, just knew it, but I couldn't prove it. I sat there feeling nervous and unsettled, but all that went away as soon as he arrived. I was so full of joy just to look at him; it was like I came alive again, I hadn't felt like that in ages.

However, he was his arrogant self, as per usual. The first thing he said was: 'You knew you were coming to see me and that's how you've dressed?'

I had on black trousers, a black top, black shoes and a leopard print cardigan. I looked at him and asked: 'What's wrong with my clothes?'

He gave me a sarcastic smile and responded: 'The fact that you have to ask shows me that there is no point in me wasting my time explaining it to you! Anyway, how is Gabriel?'

I told him Gabriel was alright, but I was annoyed with his lack of empathy for me: he never even asked how I was. He saw in my face that I wasn't 100 per cent, but I guess he just didn't care. After a while, we headed up to his therapist and, in the car, he told me I would have to wait in the car for an hour, and then I would join them for the next hour. I thought to myself: Couldn't he have told me that, and I would have come at my time instead of waiting in the car in a place where there are no shops around for me to go and entertain myself?

We got there, and he went in. After an hour, he called me to go in. His therapist came to meet me downstairs at the door, we had a small chat on the way up and, when we got to his office, I saw Patrick sat in there in a way I'd never seen him before. It wasn't the arrogant, the ugly, the nasty or the angry mask: it was vulnerability. I had never seen vulnerability in that man; he started talking about his upbringing with his mother and his grandmother, all the abuses he'd encountered in his life and the reasons he hated them so much. He also talked about his marriage and how all the women in his life betrayed him and cheated on him, and how he'd shut down completely for nine years regarding relationships and, then when he'd decided to try dating, he'd met me. He said all I did was to try to put him down, destroy him and mess up his life. He asked me what he had done to me for me to feel the need to do all the things that I had done? What were my motives? Why would I say I loved him but do things that proved otherwise? He tried to help me with Gabriel and everything, but I took it all the wrong way and reacted in ways he couldn't begin to understand.

I was dumbfounded. Looking back, I should have said: 'Excuse me? Are you kidding me? That's what you do to me? How can you sit here in front of your therapist and invent this story against me?' But the stupid, blind and in love me sat there quietly, listening to all of that, and felt bad that my love was feeling hurt due to my actions. When his therapist asked me if I had anything to say, I didn't say much, because I was overwhelmed with everything. I said: 'I never knew you felt that way. You never really showed any deep feelings towards me and it seems like everything I do is never good enough for you. Then you go off and start shouting. I don't like people shouting at me: I completely shut down …'.

He cut me off, saying, 'I don't shout at you. I might be passionate when I talk, but I don't treat you inappropriately!'

I didn't agree or disagree as I didn't want a scene in front of his therapist. But I thought to myself: You must have a short memory! Then I said: 'To be honest, Patrick, you are so disregarding of my feelings the entire time during these weeks that we haven't seen each other, I thought you probably already had someone else. You were always bragging that I should feel lucky that I have your attention, that there are better put together women out there who are financially stable and healthier to be in a relationship than I am. According to you, the only attractive things in me are my kindness, humility and the willingness to make this relationship work. Honestly, I never expected to see you again!'

While I was talking, I noticed some exchanging of awkward and tense looks between them. Again, I felt like something was wrong, and that he was hiding something from me.

I found out that night that I was right all along! He was already seeing someone else and, according to him, he was undecided as to which one he should go for. I felt so upset about it that I felt like I could punch him in the face. Why the hell did he ask me to go there that day? To hurt me even more than I already was. I could see the joy in his face talking about the other girl: how great she was, that she was also a single mother, but owned her own house, had a nice car, was a hotel manager, although she worked part-time. She was well spoken and Caribbean like him, so communication between them was easy.

I sat there listening quietly but screaming inside my head. I was in a rage but with a stupid smile on my face like I was alright with the situation. I couldn't stop smiling, and that was enraging me even more! In the end he said: 'Ah, I started having these nasty spots in my private areas and wondered when the last time was you got yourself tested?'

'Excuse me? What do you mean?'

'I mean sexual screening. I never had none of these things and I know it's the kind of thing prostitutes normally have.'

'Excuse me? WTF are you trying to say?' I asked him again, but this time I was livid.

'As far as I know, we always used protection. Plus, you are the one that's got someone else, and the one that once told me you have already slept with over 100 women. You treated sex like sport and used to sleep with three women or more in one day. So, what exactly are you trying to imply?'

He saw I was fuming, and he backed down by saying: 'I'm sure it is nothing, but it would be great to get tested. We talked about that, of doing it together, but we never did.'

I said: 'I will for sure, because now I am worried that I might have something that you have passed on to me! And since you have a new girl then you should do the same.' I picked up my stuff and stormed out of his office. The nerve this man had.

I got home and Dalila was waiting for me! She asked me what happened and if things worked out between us, and I told her about the new girl, but as usual I cut out the bad parts of the arguments and his nasty insinuation. Dalila had the information I wanted her to have; I guess I knew from the beginning that Patrick was toxic and crazy, but I was under his spell. He made me feel so invalidated that I thought I couldn't do better than him and that no one else would love and care for me and my son like he did. I felt that all the arguments and downsides of our relationship were worth it if my son could have him as a male role model in his life: an alpha male, as he would often say.

## Delusional Me

We stopped seeing each other around March 2016. I did go and take the sexual screening given my family history; I do not play with these things. I got hold of that rage I was feeling against him and used it to get over him. However, when you truly love someone, you do not get over it that easily. Then I had Dalila giving me hope by saying he was just having a rebound and eventually would be back. She didn't know half the story, but I did grab onto what she was saying because I wanted to believe in that, and I did in fact start believing it was a question of time until Patrick came back.

*'Maybe the journey isn't so much about becoming anything. Maybe it's unbecoming everything that isn't really you so you can be who you were meant to be in the first place.'*

*- Paulo Coelho -*

I took the time I was alone to analyse what was good and bad in my relationship with Patrick. I would still make excuses for his nasty behaviour at times, and it would all come down to me being the main reason he would go off like that.

I started seeing my therapist, Ian, and I continued to make changes around myself. I started to exercise every day with my friend Catarina; we would go for a run at 5.30 a.m. before work. Then one time, in conversation with my friend Beta, she told me about this detox she was doing with Arbonne products and I decided to follow her lead. Physically, I was starting to feel great, but mentally I was still fragile and vulnerable. One day, while looking for meditations and motivational videos on YouTube, I came across Wayne Dyer! I watched his videos repeatedly: Power of Intention, 101 Ways to Transform Your Life, Control Your Thought and Mind, etc. I read the books *The Power of Your Subconscious Mind, The Secret* and *The Road less Travelled.*

I also became closer to God: I felt that during my relationship with Patrick, I'd distanced myself from my father in the skies. The months I was with Patrick, eighty per cent of me was trying to figure out how to completely please him so he wouldn't be upset all the time, and the other twenty per cent was trying to co-exist between work, Gabriel and home. I started going to church again, kneeling more often for prayers, embracing silence, abstaining from social media (for a month), doing things on my own, meditating, listening more, talking less, and looking at myself in the mirror at least once a day and appreciating the person in front of me.

During this time, I started to realise that Patrick was a troubled and insecure person. But, instead of backing down and praying for him to stay away, I decided that when Patrick came back to me again, he would find a different, strong and mature woman and he would fall in love with me all over again. I was convinced that perhaps that's what he needed: someone that would show him unconditional love like his mother never did. I was convinced that inside him was a child that just needed to be loved and feel secure, and I was convinced I was going to be the woman that was going to show him that. All I needed was to learn to be patient and work on myself the way he wanted me to do. He was a good man, he just never had anyone that understood him like I did. Now that I knew what he wanted from me; things would be perfect between us.

Finally, I got my sexual screening results. I wasn't upset with him any more over his insinuation; I was sure he didn't mean any harm. I asked the nurse to give me a letter with the results instead of just receiving them over the phone, and I decided to send it to Patrick with a thank you note! On the card I wrote: 'Dear Patrick, I believe you asked for this test! As you can see, I am as clean as I can be. Hope you are alright. Thank you for everything that you have done for us, yesterday, today and tomorrow! Love always, Aurea.'

I posted it and waited with a deep certainty he would call me as soon as he received that. I sent it on a Wednesday, and he called me on Monday. I was at work. He asked me if we could talk! I said yes and he said: 'I received your card and the test results. I wasn't expecting it from you but thanks. How are you and Gabriel?' I told him we were great and that it was great to hear from him and, that he sounded happy! He responded that he wasn't that happy and started telling me about his problems with his girlfriend, that she was this and she was that. She didn't listen and just did what she wanted, that he tried to be patient. but it was driving him crazy, that things between them went so fast, that he already knew all her family, that everything looked great in the beginning but now he wasn't sure anymore. So, I cut him off and told him: 'Patrick, give the girl a chance. You always go too fast. Try to relax and enjoy the trip; stop pressuring her and yourself. Relationships take time to build!'

He went quiet for a moment and then said: 'Wow Aurea, that's very mature of you to say! Thank you, I appreciate it as I wasn't expecting you to say something like that. Anyway, how about you? Are you seeing anyone?'

I told him no, that I was taking the time to focus on myself, my son, my house... and that I was waiting on him! He went silent again, and then said: 'Aurea, I am with someone else!'

To that I said: 'I know. Do what you have to do! Things will fall into place at the right time. I understand you have to do it now. Explore what you have to explore. I can wait; I am not in a rush!'

In fact, I wasn't in a rush – I was delusional and feeding the ego of a narcissist, giving him everything he needed to continue to be his worst self.

## Living a fairy tale in my head

As I (and Dalila) expected, things went left with the other girl (around May) and he started calling me again to go out: to the cinema, to just hang out, talk, and eventually we started spending more time romantically. He noticed the changes in me, and he was happy and impressed about that. For almost a month, we were good and happy together. We would spend more time together at his house on the weekends: me, him and Gabriel while his flat mate was away. And, some weekends, just the two of us. One time we even went out with his flat mate and his girlfriend! That was a great night until Patrick started telling them things I'd told him in confidence. His friend told us he was happy to see us together again and he asked, in a joking way, what the plans were for the future. Patrick took it literally and said that there were no plans until I sorted my head, that I had many problems and he couldn't jump in there and fix them. Then he started telling his friend about my relationship with my mom, my problems with Pedro and that I was abused as a child. I felt humiliated and disappointed that things I'd told him in confidence he was telling people right there, out loud, so everyone around us could hear. He made me and his friends feel uncomfortable, but he didn't care. His flat mate had to tell him to stop, that it wasn't his place to be talking about all of that. Patrick responded by saying it was true and he didn't see any problem in telling the truth, which should always be told.

'It's not your truth and it's not the place or the time for it to be said. If Aurea wanted us to know, she would do that herself,' Frank said.

Patrick said: 'No, she wouldn't. She doesn't know how to tell the truth because she lives in a world where people live through lies!'

His mate just said: 'That's enough. Let's change the subject.'

Patrick looked at me like he was expecting me to defend him, because he was feeling like an asshole. I didn't make eye contact, because I didn't want the confrontation. Fortunately, the conversation changed in a good way, and we ended up having a great time.

Gabriel and Patrick became so attached to each other that Gabriel eventually started to transfer the love he had for his father to Patrick. To be fair, he was always great to Gabriel, and my little man always looked forward to spending weekends there with him and doing things as a family. Their ties became so strong that Gabriel even started calling him Dad. My son was happy, and I was even happier for him. I was feeling like finally we were going somewhere, that the sacrifices I was making, like isolating from my friends and being more submissive, were a good price to pay. I wouldn't talk to anyone on the phone if it was not on loudspeaker because I didn't want him to be suspicious for no reason. I would still talk to my friends, but just over the phone. I wouldn't make plans with them, because weekends were to be spent with Patrick and he didn't like to socialise, so we would just confine ourselves to his office all day. There he had two TVs, and he and Gabriel would play video games, one on each TV, and I would sit there all-day reading books or just looking at them enjoying themselves. I wouldn't go on my phone for too long, because I knew that would annoy him.

One time I said: 'Since you guys will be spending time playing video games in your office, I am arranging to go to the cinema with my friend Tuxa.' I ended up having to cancel because he told me he was waiting for me to help him with some things around the office. We didn't do anything, just things he normally would do, and then we went out for a meal. The next weekend, he had an extra TV in his office. He said he bought it for me so I could watch Netflix while they played, and I could invite my friend to come over if I wanted, as there were drinks and snacks available too. I felt uncomfortable with his attitude, but all I said was 'thank you' as I didn't want to sound ungrateful.

I also remember a weekend where Gabriel was at his uncle's house, so it was just the two of us. For some reason, Patrick was in a good mood the whole weekend. I told him I would just stay with him Friday to Saturday, as Sunday was Dalila's birthday and I was planning on taking her and the kids out to celebrate. Saturday, we were supposed to go out after I came from my therapy session, but he was into his video games and gave me the excuse that he was tired. The next morning, I got dressed to leave and he was surprised I was leaving so early. All of a sudden, he wasn't feeling well, so I felt bad leaving him. I called Dalila and said I would just wait for his mate to come home, but then would be there asap, and we could still go out. Dalila wasn't in the mood to go out, so she said not to worry, we could do that tomorrow, and today she just wanted to be home and in her pyjamas. I told her I would bring wine and food and we could stay in! I stayed at Patrick's watching him play games on his TV all morning, and when I got fed up and told him I was leaving, he got dressed and asked me if I could take him into town. We went, and I said I wanted to buy a present for Dalila. I didn't have any time to do so though as he took me to the shops he wanted to go to, and in a few of them he bought me clothes, showed me how to mix them around, and then said that was the way he expected to see me dressed every time I went to see him. At the end, he told me to change into one of my new outfits and asked me to drop him home again. I didn't want to go in, but he said: 'I just brought you clothes. Bring them in and let's have a look at them (like we haven't done that at the shop already).'

I saw what he was doing, and I was starting to get annoyed, so I said: 'Patrick, I have people waiting for me!'

'I told you this morning I wasn't feeling well, but I still took the time to go and do something nice for you. But all you seem to want to do is storm out of here.'

I felt selfish all of a sudden but manipulated at the same time. I ended up calling Dalila again and Gabriel's auntie (Maria) to ask if it was alright to pick him up the next day. I did tell Ian (my therapist) as well, and he used the word controlling to describe Patrick's behaviour.

More and more, I started to peel off Patrick layer by layer, asking myself if I was willing to really go the long haul with him. Nevertheless, I continued to pray for us, for our relationship and ask God every day to use me as a bridge between him and Patrick so I could help him see the light and the trail to LOVE.

I got Patrick an Angolan housekeeper (my friend's auntie), and she too would tell me to pray for him and tell me she was also praying for him, as she could see he wasn't a bad person but was troubled by his past, and that affected his present. She told me to get a picture of him, light a white candle every night and pray for him. She was my confidant while we were together, because she was older, spoke the same language as me and knew Patrick as I did, because around us he was himself. Around other people he was fake, cynical and charming!

Around August, we broke up again, but this time it was because I put my foot down in a situation I found extremely disrespectful. It was a Saturday night, we ordered Chinese and were having some wine. Gabriel was in bed, we were watching movies on Netflix, deciding what to watch and debating about different things and joking around. Basically, the night was going well. However, his phone kept buzzing. I didn't take much notice because he is a businessman, and I was used to people calling him late at night or early in the morning to solve problems or whatever. I was leaning on his chest and, when he went to reply to a message one of the times, I noticed he was talking with this girl and it wasn't about work. Apparently, they had been on a date already and she was asking him what he thought of her. I snapped. I was like: 'What are you doing? Who are you talking to? Who is Tina?'

He looked at me super-calm and said: 'A girl I met; we have been talking but nothing is going on.'

'I am sorry: am I missing something? So, you are seeing me and other people?'

'Well, I never said we were exclusive.'

I was in a rage, and I told him that from the moment my son was involved and started calling him Dad, we were pretty much exclusive and that if he wanted to play around, he should have told me about it so I could protect mine and my child's feelings. If he expected me to be faithful and behave seriously, I was expecting the same from him. He retaliated, saying it wasn't a problem that he was talking to other people and in fact he had been talking and going on dates with many different girls, but talking is not cheating. He said I didn't understand because I was insecure and narrow-minded, that a real and mature woman would not take much notice of that situation, but of course I had to make a scene and be dramatic. We'd had a happy day and lately things had been good he said, but I had to spoil everything because I didn't know how to be happy.

I told him to f... him and the mature women he knew. That, where I come from, all real women I knew wouldn't accept a situation like that. If he thought that just because he paid for stuff and treated my son with love, I was going to be submissive to that point, he was very much mistaken. He had never seen me like that: I had the devil inside of me. I didn't say much, but I made him understand that if he said one more word, I wouldn't be responsible for myself.

I tried to sleep, but I couldn't really. He just sat there playing video games instead. I didn't leave because it was late, and Gabriel was asleep. The next morning, as soon as I was awake, he started telling me the same old things, to invalidate me and make me feel guilty for the way I talked to him the night before.

I let him finish, then looked into his eyes with the same ugly and nasty face he gave me many times, and asked him: 'Have you finished with your bullshit? If I am all of that, why am I still here in your bed? What's the matter? You lost your game? If you are that great, why aren't you married already with a great family, huh? Ah, I know, because you are incapable of love. You are full of bullshit; you have the talk, but you don't have the walk. I might not be an alpha female, but I see you now, Patrick. You can't hide from me, and you sure are not going to humiliate or invalidate me anymore! Ask Tina to be your next victim!'

The man had no words. I'd never seen him lost for words! It felt good to say all of that, but wrong that I had to sink to his low level.

I stormed out of there in my pyjamas and with my son in my arms. He didn't know me at all: I will give all of me to the person I love, but at the first sign of betrayal you will see my ugliest side. And when that side comes out, you do not want to cross me. I was awake again, and very awake, very rageful. I was feeling very stupid for all the time I'd invested in him  and was very much ready to make a stand.

On the way home, Gabriel told me out of nowhere: 'Mom, you need to buy a princess dress so you can get married to Uncle Patrick soon!'

I said: 'Aw, Gabriel, I don't think that will ever happen; I don't think Uncle Patrick wants to marry Mom!'

'He does Mom: we went to buy you a ring the other day! Auntie Tuxa came with us and helped him choose it for you. It is really big and shiny.'

My mouth dropped open! I do remember Tuxa went to pick up Gabriel once at Patrick's office because we wanted to go out that night. I was at work and Gabriel was already on holiday from school. I do remember when I went to pick up Gabriel at her house, she was all enthusiastic about Patrick, and how great he was with Gabriel. She literally said I'd hit the jackpot with him, and she was very happy for me. For a moment I'd thought: If only you knew, my friend! But as she continued to talk, her enthusiasm actually got to me. She went on and on about how Gabriel was more confident, that he needed someone like Patrick in his life, that boys need that, and this and that, and I thought to myself: Yes, it is all worth it if my son is well!

I called Tuxa when I got home and asked her about the ring. She first pretended she didn't know anything, but then I told her Gabriel told me and she started telling me everything. I was actually annoyed with his attitude, as I could see he was trying to manipulate my friends into seeing him as some God that came to save me. It was one thing to fool me for so long, but when you come for my friends or my family, I get very defensive.

I told her everything I was going through, everything about his behaviour and how he was talking with these women. She was perplexed and couldn't believe what she was hearing. So, I told her he never had any intention of marrying me: all he wanted was one of my friends in his corner so, if I ever wanted to pull out of the relationship, she would be the one putting some sense into me to stay in a relationship with him.

She said: 'He did fool me very well. We talked for hours and it seemed like he was super in love with you and Gabriel and that he had big plans for your future together. But you know that I do not support that kind of behaviour from a man. My friend, run for your life: this man is crazy, let him go; you deserve better. He can be good to Gabriel, but he also needs to be good to you and not just pretend to others, and then between four walls he is treating you like an object that he moves around according to his suitability. He is playing with your feelings. That is very, very mean; this man has no heart!'

I couldn't have agreed more with her. She told me to be strong and avoid contact with him, so I did.

After a couple of days, he sent an email to my work account. He had my personal email, but I knew he was doing that to emotionally disturb me. I read it very calmly and, as usual, it was full of arrogance, domineering and trashy words; all with the purpose of making me feel bad and guilty for putting my foot down and standing my ground.

I emailed him back, basically saying: 'Dear Patrick, please understand that I was with you because I loved you and the way you took and loved my child; not because you are an Idris Elba lookalike, not because of your nice house, or money, your business or whatever else you think you are great at. In fact, at this point I actually ask myself why I fell for you so stupidly… Being with you is not easy and you must agree with me! It's isolating, it's overwhelming, it's confusing and frustrating most, if not all, the time. With you, everything is your way or the highway: it's manipulative and hurtful. What you call your truth when talking to me is just pure rage and hurtful words. I am never good enough for you, but the fact is you love to have me around. Why? Does it give you pleasure to put me down with your so-called truth? Do you think I don't know if I stay with you or even get married (yes, Gabriel told me about the ring) to you my life will be lonely? I am sure that if we ever get to that stage, I would be spending holidays on my own with Gabriel because you would probably be too busy or not bothered to leave your office and your video games to spend time with us. From what I could see from the last time in your house, I would probably spend most of my nights alone because you would probably be entertaining other women because that fulfils your ego. The thing is, I don't cheat, and I don't expect to be cheated on. I know you think of yourself as a Greek God that women can't resist and that time is running out for me, and I should be happy that I have got your attention. Guess what? Time is also running out for you and, so you know, you are not that great, and I am starting to understand why you have been single all these years.'

In response, he called me Mean Spirit Girl! (laughs), and said it was time for me to find a man at my level, because he could see I struggled with whatever he was trying to teach me. He said that, due to my environment and my willingness to stay stuck to it, I would never be able to evolve or see the bigger picture. However, at the bottom of the email, he said that despite all that, he did love Gabriel and, if I was up for it, he would like to spend time with him and help him with subjects that only a man can. He understood if I needed time and space, given the situation, but to think of what was best for Gabriel and put my feelings aside.

I took a moment to think about everything and forwarded all the emails we exchanged between us to Tuxa, with a note saying: 'There you go, as transparent and crazy as I told you he was! Is this an email from a man that had intentions of marrying me? At least this time I have proof!'

Of course, there were many more things he and me said in the emails, but I don't remember any more. But I was happy that, this time, I had something to show people.

That was another thing with Patrick: he would say things and, when I would bring it up, he would say he never said anything like that. He would say I was crazy or that wasn't what he said but, because I never listened, I got mixed-up and became stupid, immature and childish. I remember one time he told me he was going to buy a new bed, and I saw him looking at beds online. The next day I asked him if he bought the bed, and he looked at me like I was crazy and told me his bed was in perfect condition, so why would he buy a new bed? For the rest of the night, he would occasionally look at me, laugh annoyingly and call me crazy and coocoo.

Another time he told me to come over during the week because he fancied going out for dinner, and perhaps cocktails. I showed up at his office looking flawless, and he looked me up and down and asked me where I was going dressed like that. I told him I was going out with him, but he said he was not going anywhere: he had already eaten, he said, and was having his chill time playing video games with an online friend and didn't want to be disturbed.

I looked at him and said: 'But Patrick, you called me and you told me to come over so we could go out!'

He looked straight in my face and said very arrogantly: 'No I didn't. Are you crazy? Oh, I know! You have so many men that you can't keep track of who and when?' He turned his back and went straight to his game leaving me standing there wondering if I dreamed about it or if I was actually crazy. I found myself at times asking the same question over and over again of him (which would annoy him), and even texting him so I then had proof he did say or ask something. Our texts and emails were always gigantic, so I made sure I covered all bases and to avoid arguments next time I saw him.

This time his words were there in black and white. It seems stupid, but that gave me joy to know that he couldn't run away from that (like he cared).

Tuxa once again said that she was lost for words, and I have never seen that woman lost for words! She told me to try to move on, but that she agreed it would be good for Gabriel to continue to see him because she could see how good he was with him, and how much Gabriel had come out of his shell since I was with Patrick. I didn't show Dalila the emails, but I told her some of what had happened, but basically, she thought me and him were finishing because of the other women. I told her about the ring, and she continued to say that eventually he was coming back, that maybe he just had cold feet. So, I let her believe in whatever she was believing, but didn't explain much to her or my friend Beta. I wasn't ready to tell them all the truth: I didn't want them to see me as weak and stupid. They were my closest friends at the time, and I couldn't bear having them looking at me differently or even asking me questions I wasn't ready to respond to. Tuxa, on the other hand, was different: she is a good listener and she has a way of making you talk without feeling judged or on the spot.

Dalila didn't agree with Patrick still seeing Gabriel. She and my friend Carlinha were the only ones that told me that if me and Patrick were finished for good, I had no business letting him have any influence in Gabriel's life. They even asked me what would happen if I found someone else? It was bad enough the person having to deal with a father; now there would also be the almost-stepfather.

Deep down, I knew they were right, but I felt I owed that to Gabriel. He had a non-present father, and his connection with Patrick was too deep for me to just break it up. I felt I needed time to see how everything was going to pan out before I brought it up with my son. Honestly, I was trying to protect my son's feelings and emotional well-being. The question was, could I trust Patrick to keep his word? What would happen if he found someone? How would they take to him still bonding with my child? And how about me finding someone else? How would he take it?

I brought all of this to him and, as usual, he gave an arrogant answer, saying he wasn't irrational or emotional like I was, so he couldn't see any problems in that arrangement. This was all about Gabriel and nothing to do with me, him or us, and as far as he was concerned, us didn't exist anymore.

*'Stupid is knowing the truth, seeing the truth, but still believing in lies…'*

-     *Reas Kuron –*

## Travelling with friends, the best Therapy in the World

I compromised with Patrick, taking Gabriel to spend time with him every Saturday afternoon while I was at my therapy sessions! I used to dress my best, put my make-up on and I would refuse to go into his office when dropping off Gabriel. Everything was very practical, kind and 'professional. As my therapist said: 'Keep the encounters with him short and sweet; don't give him time to say or do anything that will put you down. Be polite but be mysterious and don't give much away. It's not his business what you are going to do the rest of the day.'

After a couple of weeks, I was travelling to New York with my friends Elizabeth and Carla, and I was going to meet my other friend there (Carlinha). So, I had to tell him that for two weekends Gabriel wasn't going, as I was going to be travelling, and I wasn't going to ask Dalila to go out of her way to bring Gabriel to him as she was already doing me a great favour taking care of him while I was away. Patrick immediately offered to have Gabriel to stay for the weekends as, in his own words: 'that would give Gabriel a break from the girls!' I asked Gabriel if he would like that and he said yes.

So, I made my arrangements with Dalila, gave Patrick her number and vice versa, and told Dalila she wasn't to take Gabriel to him. If he wanted to have him on the weekend, he should come to pick him up, as I knew she was super-busy during the weekends with her catering business, so didn't want to mess her around. All was sorted for me to go! However, on the day I was supposed to travel, minutes before entering the plane, I called Dalila one last time and she told me Patrick had changed the plans for that weekend. His excuse was that something came up and he could not make it to pick up Gabriel.

I texted him straight away to say that if it was going to be like that the next weekend, he better let me know then, so I could arrange something else with another person as Dalila had something arranged already as she thought I had everything covered with Gabriel. His arrogant self texted me back to say that he too had made plans for Saturday, and it was something that couldn't wait until the following week. I knew what he was trying to do, so I just texted Dalila back and said: 'You are responsible for Gabriel, if you think you should sort something else instead of relying on him then ask Maria for me please. He is trying to ruin my holidays and I already have the feeling that the only reason he wants to be involved in Gabriel's life is to make me be or feel like I am stuck with him and that I need to be as grateful as I can be because he is doing me a favour. But he is not going to control or dictate my life like that.'

Dalila agreed with me. She also told me 'I told you so', but she was my friend and trying to understand where I was coming from and be supportive of my decisions. In the end I told her: 'You are his mom now; I trust that you will do what's best for Gabriel!'

Travelling with your friends has a magical power! If things are bad, it brings you healing. If they are great, it brings you experiences and knowledge, awakens you to the wonders of the world. It deepness your friendships and shows you how much you don't know and still need to know about your friends. I was with three strong-minded women, all in search of something. I think, apart from Carla, we were all going through something. Beta was trying to come to terms with her mother passing away, Carlinha was having a break from her job as it was affecting her emotionally (she is a social worker) and I was trying to figure out who I was and why I'd been ignoring so many red flags, I let myself fall for an emotionally unavailable and damaged man like Patrick. I was trying to understand my neediness for love and how to disconnect from Patrick without hurting Gabriel. I knew I couldn't keep seeing Patrick: I had come to an understanding in therapy that just because you love someone does not mean that you have to like them. Every time I thought about the way he treated me or made me feel in the past, I would dislike him more and more. But when I would think on his relationship with Gabriel, my heart would soften again.

If you see my pictures from New York, my eyes always look distant, lost and full of emotions. Decisions, decisions, decisions. However, I was surrounded by love, loyalty, trust. I felt safe to be me, to share my emotions and some of my struggles, but I still felt stupid, to be honest about all the emotional abuse I endured with Patrick. These women saw in me as a strong woman with a strong personality. However, I felt like a fraud everywhere I went, and especially among them. Looking back, I should have taken up to them: I was in a safe place, with safe people (my people) but I didn't trust myself to let them have my secrets, and still love me the same way. I was afraid of what they would say or of them judging me.

To Carla, Beta and Carlinha: I apologise for what you guys didn't know and for doubting your understanding and love for me. It has nothing to do with any of you, but all to do with me. Nevertheless, we had a good time: we laughed, we cried, we argued, we played like children, we had fun. On my birthday, they spoiled me with so many surprises, and they even had me crying in the middle of New York by having Gabriel on FaceTime singing happy birthday to me! That was my first birthday away from my son, but it was the one when I felt the most connected to myself (to my soul). I was away from my surroundings, so it helped me put things into perspective. I was feeling like I was out of my bubble, therefore, I could see inside of it, analyse what needed to be changed, what needed to be added and what needed to be kept the same. Every day I would ask God to bring before me those who were worthy of my love and to save/protect me from those that were here to hurt/deceive me.

On our last night in New York, I dreamed about Patrick. We were in a small boat in the middle of a lake and it was dark and cold, and he told me he couldn't see me anymore. In the dream, I asked him what about Gabriel? And he responded: 'Gabriel as well. I can't see any of you anymore.' All of a sudden, I was out of the boat and on the land with a wedding dress on, and he was still on the boat in the middle of the lake, but his spirit was very tormented, and it seemed like he was having an internal battle. I stood there observing him going through his internal fight and I felt relieved that I was no more a part of it. I then started walking in the direction of the sunrise and, all of a sudden, Gabriel was holding my hand, the sunlight was in our faces. It was a nice warm feeling and we were content and peaceful. We looked at each other and we smiled and then I told him: 'It's just the two of us but we are going to be just fine!'

I woke up, however, a bit tormented by my dream, perhaps because I didn't manage to speak with Dalila the day before. I told my friends about the dream; Beta is like me, so she knew it meant something, but she was sure it was something great. Both Carlas are more in the scientific spectrum, so they couldn't understand why I was so agitated with my dream. Eventually, I stopped to think and take deep breaths, and I was suddenly invaded by this warm feeling that God was telling me in advance that everything was going to be all right: 'This too, shall pass!'

So, I spent the rest of the day enjoying the last day of a trip of my lifetime!

## 'I see you'

The day I arrived back from New York, Dalila wasn't at home, so I took the time to unpack and call Patrick to let him know that I didn't think it was wise to keep the arrangement. I was going to give him and Gabriel a couple more weekends while I started preparing him for the break-up. I apologised for any inconvenience but told him I thought that was for the best.

As expected, he started going off on me, saying he was expecting that from me because I am a selfish person – I am irrational and emotional, therefore I was predictable. I told him perhaps he was right, but it was what it was, and I needed to think of everything for the long-term.

He wanted to stay with Gabriel overnight, but I told him I was coming to pick him up as I missed my son. In the meantime, Dalila came home. I told her about the holiday, showed her pictures and then asked her about Gabriel and the communication with Patrick. For some reason, I could sense something happened while I was away. She told me she didn't really believe he was staying with Gabriel to help him, but because of me. That they'd had long and exhausting conversations on the phone almost every day while I was gone. That he very bluntly asked her about her situation and why she ended up living with me, and then talked about me in a way that made her feel uncomfortable. He told her about my abuse and private things me and him had talked about and told her she didn't really know me: I was crazy, irrational and having conversations with me or making me understand things was painful.

She also told me that in most of their conversations, he used to compare me to his mother. She believed that, in his mind, I was his mother, Gabriel was him as a child and he was one of his stepfathers that he loved very much. According to him, he and his stepfather had a great relationship: he called him Dad and they loved each other. But his crazy mother screwed the man's life and he ended up walking out on them and never came back. That, on top of everything she had done to him, was one more thing he would never forgive her for.

I told Dalila I came to the same realisation myself, that in most of our arguments I was always left with a sense that after a certain point he wasn't talking to me anymore, but with his mother. And when I would ask him what he was talking about, he would get even more aggressive and tell me that I didn't listen, that's why I am crazy and stupid. I learned with time to just let him vent; eventually he would get tired and switch over to something else on TV or something else would pop up in his mind.

Dalila then touched on the subject of the abuse and asked me if it was true. I felt unprepared and put on the spot. I wasn't upset with Dalila but with Patrick: who the hell did he think he was to be sharing my story and my truth with my friend. If I didn't share with her, it is because I didn't feel prepared to do so, so who was he to take that away from me? I hated him in that moment. I knew what he was trying to do with Dalila, and I hoped that she realised that too: he was trying to set her against me and show her that I wasn't a person to be trusted. He even said to her that a person that keeps too many secrets is not one to be trusted.

I didn't say much to her about my abuse, only that it was something in the past and was something I tried to overcome on my own terms and now through therapy. I haven't told anyone really and I talked to him because he went through so much as a child, and I thought he could understand without looking at me with pity. I was very disappointed he brought that to her without my consent. and as a weapon to make her feel like she shouldn't trust me.

She told me not to worry about that: she wasn't stupid and understood the game straight away because her ex tried that with a few of her friends. They try to isolate you or pit your mates against you so, in the end, you feel they are the only person you have around.

She also told me I should look again at the situation of him having Gabriel sometimes. She didn't want to interfere in my life and my decisions, but it was her obligation, as a mother and a friend, to let me know he was changing Gabriel, in a bad way. She was starting to see a little of Patrick in Gabriel. He was becoming arrogant towards everyone at home, disrespectful toward the girls, had a big sense of entitlement and made sexist comments. She told me she'd had two situations where she had to tell him off and ask where he'd heard that, and he'd said he heard it from Uncle Patrick.

I was finally getting all the last pieces of the puzzle I needed. Of course, a narcissist like Patrick had other motives when offering to be Gabriel's mentor. He inflicting on my child all the hate he had for women. Because he hated his mother, he would probably eventually start making my son hate me. Patrick obviously didn't know me. I guess he thought that because he could manipulate me all this time, I wouldn't see that. I saw certain behaviour in Gabriel with the girls before I travelled, and I wasn't happy with it. I remember mentioning it to Patrick and asking him to have a word with him on how a boy/man should address a girl/woman; and his response was: 'You ever thought if he reacted like that it was because he felt undermined by them? You women like to do that with men – cut the boy some slack.'

That was the day I started feeling he wasn't the best mentor for my son and that although Gabriel loved him, that relationship wouldn't work long-term for me or Gabriel, only for Patrick. He probably saw my son as a lab rat he could manipulate and grow into a damaged man and a woman-hater like himself.

I told Dalila she was right, that I wasn't feeling right about it either and he was already aware of it. I could see she wanted to ask or say more things, but she didn't. Perhaps she didn't have the courage to do so or just thought it was the wrong time. But she finished by saying that he still wanted me, that she'd told him that too and he didn't deny it. She told him that he could keep having other women, but he wouldn't find what he loved in me. Although I wasn't the fantasy woman he had created in his head, I had for sure more or all the qualities for a good wife and partner. She told him he made a huge mistake by taking me for granted and expecting me to bow my head to everything because he thought he was in control. She let him know that I was independent before I met him and, no matter what, I knew that if everything else failed I was going to be OK. I had done it once, so I could do it twice. She told him losing him didn't scare me as I had nothing to lose, but he sure had loads to lose.

I sat there and contemplated her words. I don't know if she really said that to him, but her words got into my head and my heart with the greatest power. I needed to hear it, as I'd never thought like that. I never thought that I was going to be OK, I knew I needed to get my distance from him and stop the visitations, but I was dreading it deep down because I still loved him. Honestly, I think that deep down I still believed that eventually he would come to the realisation of what he'd lost, that he would see he needed to change his ways and would come and look for us.

But my rational side knew that was never going to happen, that we were done and needed to be done for my mental health's sake. I never stopped to think how I would cope after things were 100 per cent done between us. Dalila reminded me that I was strong, a fighter, and I wasn't really losing anything because I didn't have anything with him. We didn't build anything together and there was nothing left: just my love for him and a bag full of pain, humiliation, self-doubt, rejection, depression, lack of love, mental abuse, constant guilt, lack of confidence, isolation, fear, low self-esteem, anxiety and lies to my friends. It was time to leave that negative weight behind me.

I went to pick up Gabriel, and all my attention was on him. Patrick tried to make conversation, but I pretended I was in a rush. I just wanted to get out of there, go home and enjoy my child and rest from the trip. On the way back, I asked Gabriel all sorts of question and he seemed his happy and healthy self. When I got home, Patrick texted me to say Gabriel's iPad was still there, and I told him I would come the next day to pick it up, as I wouldn't have time in the week ahead.

When I got there, I had to wait in the car, as he was late from therapy. Then I thought he would bring it to the car, but he asked me to go up, because he needed to tell me a few things. I went in and he said: 'I didn't have the chance to tell you happy birthday yesterday, so I wanted to take the chance today and give you your birthday present from me and Gabriel! I was going to ask him to do a card but I didn't have a chance!'

My thought was: 'My birthday was a week ago. He has my number, why didn't he text me? That would've been enough.' I opened the box and he'd bought me three beautiful bags from Fossil, and I knew they were not cheap. I told him he didn't have to do that, but he said he just wanted to buy me something nice for my birthday. I gave him a hug and said thank you and I noticed he felt uncomfortable and vulnerable.

When I picked up my things to leave, he told me he needed to tell me something about Dalila, if I had time to chat. I told him that if it was something I needed to know, of course, but I should have known better by then! He basically tried to trashy mouth Dalila to me, using everything she told him about herself. He even dared to say I should consider letting her go from my house because she had so many problems and could create a toxic environment, and that was not healthy for Gabriel.

I had to tell him that Dalila had been my strength during those last months, that whatever he was saying about her, I knew, because I was there. I saw her going through all her battles and she saw mine. I said that Dalila was way more patient and loving with the kids than me, and if at the moment my house was still functioning, it was because she was there with us. She might sound coocoo at times, I said, but she was a good mother – caring, responsible, rational – and I didn't appreciate him talking about her in that way. He saw he couldn't get to me that way, so he tried: 'I don't really think you should trust her with Gabriel either!'

Now he got me concerned, so I asked: 'Why? Did Gabriel complain about something?'

'No, he didn't! But I went to pick him up and he was dressed like a homeless kid, but her children were looking fine. And to be fair, me and her had many long conversations; it's clear she is going through a lot. She shouldn't be taking care of any children now because her head is not in the right place.'

I looked at him and said: 'Ah yes, her kids would be better off in the system, being fostered by strangers! Again Patrick, leave Dalila alone; the kids are fine, and she will also be fine. She just needs time to sort her stuff and get back on her feet. If you are so concerned about her, give her a good paying job: that's what she needs right now. Plus, she will stay in my house until she thinks it's suitable for her financially to move out. So far, I have no reasons to do otherwise.'

'I can see you are still tired from your trip, so whatever I am saying to you is not sinking in!'

'I am still tired, but whatever you are saying is sinking in just fine. I am used to you doing that already. Getting to know people's pains, problems or secrets and then using that against them or throwing it in their faces all the time. I am telling you that it's not working.'

'All right, all right, I can see what is happening here! You two talked about me already, didn't you? What did she say? I am sure she said negative things about me because that's what you women do.'

I looked at him and said: 'She didn't say anything that I didn't already know! BTW, who gave you the right to tell her about my abuse? Did you ask for my permission? And if you want to know, she came to the same realisation as I did ages ago: that you think I am your mother, that Gabriel is you as a child, and that you are your stepfather (the one you loved), and also that you hate women because you hate your mother. See she is not as coocoo as you think she is. A couple of conversations on the phone with you and she's got you real good... it took me nine months to realise all of that!'

He started to get all agitated and shouted: 'What did you say, bitch?'

I said: 'Your mother might have been a bitch, but I am not one, so don't call me that!'

He then looked at me with a very upset face and said: 'I want to terminate this conversation, because you are making me feel uncomfortable!'

I said: 'As you wish, but I have a question. Why did you put on a show with my friend, Tuxa, taking her to help you choose a ring that you had no intention of giving me?'

'I wanted to show you the ring and then tell you: work to be the woman that deserves it! That when I put that on your finger, I could be sure that you were the one, because you had done your work and we were now at same level in life.'

I thought: 'Wow.' I was speechless after that, at how mean that sounded. And I felt so glad that he never showed me the ring, because I was sure that in the state of mind I was before, I would have probably humiliated myself to the core just to have it. Wow, wow, wow. Patrick showed his true colours in that moment, and I was definitely sure that although I still loved him, I didn't want him anymore. I didn't like him anymore, either. His domineering words gave me a chill in my spine, and his arrogant tone and the coldness in his eyes made me feel super-uncomfortable.

I picked up my things and told him I had to leave as Dalila was waiting for me. All of a sudden, he was soft again, asking me if I wanted to eat, as he had a few more things he wanted to discuss with me. I asked him if it was about Gabriel, and he said no, but it was things about us that we needed to run over. I told him from the moment I saw his message to Tina or whatever, and when he finished with me over an email, I completely got the message and didn't think there was anything else to discuss. Out of nowhere, he started telling me not to worry about Tina because she was crazy and a waste of time. I stopped him: 'Why are you talking to me about Tina? I don't give a shit; she is not my problem…'.

'I was just trying to make you see ...'.

Before he finished, I said: 'Got to go. I don't have to be here hearing about what went wrong with the same person you were cheating on me with.'

He then said the reason he felt like he needed to go and meet other women was because he didn't feel he could trust me. Because I was secretive, that made him feel insecure and not relate at all to our relationship.

Again, I was speechless! I thought: So, it was my fault? Is he expecting me to apologise? OMG! So much manipulation, how come I never saw this before? How blind and desperate was I?

'I know it must be difficult for you to hear all of this, but I needed you to understand where I was coming from,' he said.

I just went quiet, and I could see the joy in his face. I had learned that, with people like that, you let them think that they've won and then you walk away. They are masters in manipulation and, if you try to play their game, you lose, because they are professionals at what they do. I started making my move to go and he looked confused. I am sure he thought I was going to stay over and try to gain his love back. Hell no!

'You're leaving?' he said.

'Yes, I came for an iPad and overstayed. However, it was nice to clarify some things.'

'All right. When are you bringing the little man again?'

'Well next weekend we will enjoy ourselves and spend some quality time together. Then I can bring him the week after, just for a couple of hours. I will be cutting the hours and prepare him slowly for the break-up.'

'So, you still have that in your head? I suggest you ask him straight how he would feel instead of making decisions for him: that is the kind of thing that makes children not trust their parents.'

'I will. Thanks.' And I left!

## Breaking free from your spell

Two weeks later, Patrick texted me to ask if I had thought about him continuing to see Gabriel, and if he was coming at the weekend. I told him Gabriel was happy to go for the day but, in his own words, he didn't want to go every weekend. That was perfect from my point of view, as it would make it easier to start cutting the contact with Patrick. As it was half-term, we agreed I could take Gabriel on the Friday, before work, and pick him up after.

The day before, he texted me to say he broke his finger in the gym and wouldn't be able to have Gabriel to stay. I called him afterwards to find out how he was, and he was still in the hospital with his personal trainer. He was in so much pain that his personal trainer ended up having to talk to me. He told me he had to go soon, and that there was no one to stay with Patrick. He knew me, knew I cared for Patrick, so he asked me if I could go to be with him until he could go home. I told me I would have to sort Gabriel first, but I would go ASAP.

When I got there, I found Patrick at his most vulnerable and in extreme pain. He was trying to hold it together, but it was obvious! Both he and his personal trainer were happy to see me. Even though he was in pain, he was concerned about disappointing Gabriel and failing in his promise to see him. So, I told him if he was going home that night, I would pick up Gabriel and we would stay with him for the weekend, just to keep an eye on him and help him until Monday when his housekeeper and his mate were around. I could see happiness in his face at the thought of it!

Gabriel ended up having to stay with my friend, as we left the hospital late. But the next day I asked to work from home, picked Gabriel up and some clothes, and we stayed with Patrick as promised. I was there as a friend, with no expectations whatsoever, but I could see that for everyone else it was like we were back together. His mate came back earlier that weekend with his girlfriend, and they were happy to see me there. They also assumed we were back together, and Patrick didn't deny or confirm it. I just laughed at whatever they would joke or imply, as I didn't know myself. I knew I was there with the right intentions, but I could also see myself being dragged again slowly into the cobwebs. My son was happy to be there, seeing both of us together, and spoiling Patrick with cuddles and vice versa. Patrick was being kind, respectful, considerate, patient and friendly toward me, and I was enjoying being around him.

Despite the situation, we had a nice weekend. We had to leave on Sunday afternoon, and I could see that he was sad about it. I got home and I had a nice text from him, appreciating my help but saying that he was also feeling annoyed because we left a feeling of emptiness in him and he didn't know how to deal with that on top of everything else that was happening. It was nice to hear that: it was nice to see he still had a heart somewhere in him. Perhaps I should have also considered that he was taking loads of strong painkillers. But the heart believes in what it wants to believe – I was enjoying the moment; it was finally like my prayers were heard and he realised I was the one for him. We even talked about that, and he said he never thought I would be the one to show up to help him. He thought it would be any other person or 'friends' that he had. I told him (and I stand by it) that although I was disappointed and upset with him for many reasons, it wasn't enough to refuse him help when he most needed it. But, at the same time, I am like that with everyone, and he shouldn't take it as a compliment but as one of my qualities (or curses).

As he had to have a surgery during the week to fix the bone in his finger, I was there again for him to pick him up after the surgery, take him home and keep him company. The weekend after, we went again, but this time it was just us, as his friend was out all weekend. Although it was pleasant, I started to feel isolated again. I looked around – my son was happy, Patrick seemed content, but I wasn't. I don't know what it was, but I felt suffocated. The whole weekend was on his terms: when to eat, what to eat, what to watch on TV, what to talk about, what to drink, when to sleep, when to chill, when to have a shower, when to go shopping. I just wanted to scream, but I was being patient and letting and Gabriel be happy for one more time. Patrick had an appointment at the hospital that week, and I was regretting already having offered my help to drive him there. I was missing my space, my thoughts, my wants and my own decisions. He was taking way too much space again, and I was feeling the urge to regain it.

After the weekend, I went back midweek to stay over and to take him to the hospital the day after. When I arrived at his office, he was stressed about finances and having to move out of his apartment because his mate had decided to live with his girlfriend. That was the moment I realised the man that used to talk like money was no object was living on credit. His company wasn't doing well enough to pay for his extravagance.

He told me in the beginning he rented that apartment and his friend moved there after divorcing his wife. But it was, in fact, the other way around. I remember asking him once what would happen if his mate decided to live with his girlfriend, and he said his friend would have to move out as the contract was in his name and they would have to search for something else. Slowly, lies he told me started to unfold, and also more of his personality. He would be super-nice to his mate, but then talk about him like he was a piece of shit. He even said once: 'How dare he ask me to move out so his bitch can move in. They will never last; they are two needy people living in a fantasy world. I don't give them a year!'

I didn't see any of that. What I saw were two mature people in love and wanting to spend their lives together. What's wrong with that? I made a joke and said: 'Seems like you're jealous.'

'Jealous? Of what? Them? Please, look at them and look at me! They have nothing for me to be jealous of!'

That same night after we got to his house, I noticed Patrick started to approach me more romantically. I could see that feeling upset about having to move out in a month while recovering from a broken finger was making him stressed and vulnerable. It came to a point where he said: 'I need some cuddles; I need your cuddles!'

'I can give you that,' I told him with a friendly smile on my face.

We ate and talked about many things, while looking for apartments for him. There was a moment where I thought how nice it was to be here with him and for him. But, straight away, I remembered I was always going to be happy to be there for him, but not with him anymore. I guess it is true what they say: when a person decides to leave you, it is because they've already finished that relationship with you mentally, ages ago. As I thought that, he asked me: 'Since we finished, have you been with someone else?'

Ah! The moment I was secretly awaiting – when you start to get to know the player, you start to understand the game!

'Yes,' I replied.

'Really? Who?' he asked, surprised.

'Why do you ask, and why do you want to know?'

'I am just curious! As it's nice to see your being honest about it!'

So, I said: 'I see! Well, it was the young man I had a 'fling' with before. He texted me out of the blue one day, after you finished with me over email. Normally, I would just ignore him, but that day I thought why not? I am a free woman.'

'So, are you guys together now?'

'If I was with him, I wouldn't be here with you, taking care of you and spending weekends with you,' I replied a bit offended.

'Well, we're not having sex; you're just helping me out.'

'I still think it would be disrespectful for my new man. I could probably care and come say hi, or visit, but I wouldn't spend the night or weekends with you.'

He went silent for a while, and I just stayed on my phone minding my own business. He then walked around the house a bit frantic, went for a smoke, had a drink, then came and sat next to me again. That dance of his wasn't new to me! He was upset, wanted to shout, mouth-trash me, domineer me and put me down. But he felt my vibe: I was comfortable in my own skin, didn't feel shame when I told him about my sexual encounter with my friend, and honestly it was none of his business anymore.

So, I let him do him, and I ignored the dance that before used to freak me out and made me fear what was coming next I felt powerful because I didn't feel frightened: I had nothing to lose any more. In fact, I never had, but before, I thought of him like the MAN that came to save me and make me and my son happy. Now, he was just a man! One with loads of issues and I was done trying to fix them or believing my love was enough for both of us.

He saw my contempt for his actions, so he changed his tactic and came to cuddle with me again. He didn't ask me about it again, but he turned the situation into being more romantic and we ended up having sex. I am not innocent in that; I can't act like I didn't see it coming. In fact, I wasn't sure when he started kissing me, but then I felt like I needed it to happen, like I needed closure or whatever. Honestly, I am glad it happened! It made me realise that even the sex was boring. All the sparkle I used to feel was because I was in a fantasy world and, as they say, when you are having sex with the person you love, you sometimes feel sparkles where they don't exist.

Looking back, even the sex was controlling. It would always be when he pleased, on his terms. If I wanted to express myself or talk about it, he would somehow make me feel like a whore. I remember one time, I bought this sexy lingerie, and he made me take it off and put on normal pyjamas. The rest of the night, he made jokes about how my secret dream was to be a prostitute. I started that night trying to do something nice for my man and ended up humiliated and feeling ashamed of my sexiness. Sex was basic between us; I knew it wasn't great, but I enjoyed it because I loved him. But I was starting to have a clear picture of who I was, what I liked, gaining my voice back, and I wasn't prepared to lose it again. Before, I thought I needed a man to make me feel sexy and provocative, but now I know it's already in me. It's not about him or any other man: it's about how comfortable I feel in my own skin.

This is going to sound mean, but the entire time we were having sex that night, I felt bored! All I could think about was the night I had with Ted (the young guy). That kiss that leaves you wanting for more, those big hands all over my body, him putting me up against the wall and kissing me all over my body, our bodies against each other, feeling the heat, the passion, the hungriness for each other, the heavy breathing, the desire in our eyes. Two horny human beings looking for some comfort in each other: no love, no judgements and no expectations, just pure moments of letting off steam and desire. He was going through some stuff and so was I. We were there for each other in that moment and it felt damn good. That moment with Ted brought my femininity, sexiness and self-value back. It reminded me that I do enjoy sex and that, between four walls, people should be free to explore whatever they feel comfortable to. They should talk or address everything with no judgements and no shame. I believe in the saying: 'A lady on the street and a whore for my man!'

Patrick made me go to a place where I believed that to be a good woman, I had no business showing desire for him, that sex was only for when he looked for me, that showing too much sexual interest made me a bad woman and wanting to talk about it with him made me less of a lady. This is the type of man that gives 'salad' to his woman to eat every day, and then gets himself a side-chick and eats 'beef' with her every day. I should have understood it when he told me that, when he was married, he had a lover and sometimes would also pay prostitutes. According to him, the wife and the mistress would do his head in, but with the prostitute he had the luxury of paying for silence. They would do what he wanted them to do and then leave without making a fuss. Like I said in the beginning, all the red flags were there – I just chose to make excuses for them.

The next morning, we woke up and started getting ready for the hospital appointment. I was my normal self, despising the night before. Patrick was moody and quiet. I didn't take much notice, apart from thinking he was probably in pain. On the way to the hospital, he said: 'I don't know how I feel about you sleeping with your friend!'

'What do you mean? Are you upset? Why? I am sure you've slept with many women, but as you can see, I haven't asked, because it doesn't matter! Fact is, I didn't cheat.'

'I don't see it like that! The women I sleep with are not people from my past. You had this young man on a 'shelf' for emergency sex all this time. And who's to tell me that all this time you haven't been doing that! And how am I going to look when other people find out about this.'

I started laughing and then I said: 'Is that what you did to me, when you finished with Felicia? Because I don't do that – I didn't even have his number anymore: he texted me and then called and one thing led to another. Plus, my sexual life isn't anyone else's business and I only told you because you say you like the truth, but it seems like you don't know how to handle it! Anyway, we're here (hospital). We are a bit late, so you should make a move while I'm parking the car!'

After his appointment finished at the hospital, we headed to his office! He had the same attitude. I had work to do so I did what I had to do and then I told him I had to leave, as I had parents' evening. He cornered me when I was picking up my things, and the way he was staring at me actually scared me. I asked him what was wrong, and he said: 'I can't believe that you are just going to leave like that!'

'Like what? I have things to do, and whatever I had to do here today, I have done it. You seem to be all right now, and your housekeeper is back tomorrow. You will be fine.'

He started shouting: 'I am not talking about that!'

'Why are you shouting, and what are you talking about then?'

'OMG, you are trying to defy me after everything you have done. You have no shame in what you have done? Sleeping with a kid and then throwing it in my face?'

'Patrick, you are not my boyfriend. Sex with THE KID was consensual, and he is twenty-five! Ashamed of what? I didn't look for it: it came to me, and I said yes. Plus, I didn't throw it in your face. You asked, and I told you the truth. Don't try to make it nasty, because it really wasn't and you are not going to guilt me into it. I am good with whatever happened,' I said while exiting the office.

He had to open the gates in the office because the guard was gone. I could see he wanted to blow up big time, but I was on my way out and went as fast as I could. As I got in the car and then passed the gate, I asked him: 'Are we good?'

'Think it through! What the hell do you think?' he shouted.

I said alright and left. I wasn't in the mood for whatever pathetic scene he was trying to make. If it was anyone else, I would probably have felt a bit guilty that he was upset. But after everything that he'd put me through, I had no care for what he was feeling. In fact, what I thought when he said that was: 'Whatever, bye!' And I got out of there as fast as I could.

That same night I texted him, to tell him how well Gabriel was doing at school (as per his request).

He texted back saying how proud he was of him and to pass on his message to Gabriel. Straight after, he jumped again to the same conversation we were having in the afternoon. I took the opportunity to tell him I never thought he would care who I was sleeping with, since I knew he was sleeping with all of Birmingham since he finished with me (or probably while he was with me). He then called me. Everything he was saying was meant to have me crying and be in despair begging for his forgiveness, trying to create guilt and shame, make me feel or look like a whore. He even tried to make me feel like a bad mother by asking what Gabriel or Pedro would think of it if they knew. Errrr, FOR REAL?!

But he got nothing back from me. I told him I could see where he was coming from, given the fact I knew the guy already, but everything else he was saying was bullshit, and I didn't feel guilty or ashamed about it.

'You did it to hurt me! I never saw that coming. I never thought you could hurt me, but you proved me wrong. You are evil, the worst evil I've ever encountered in my entire life!' and he hung up.

I tried to call but there was no answer, so I left it, but I did think: 'I could feel sorry for him, feel sorry because he is hurt, but I am not! In fact, I think he is being too dramatic. He never acknowledged my feelings the entire time I was with him. Every time I would become emotional, he would make fun of me, humiliate me or call me dramatic and manipulative. So why should I now feel sorry for him? Telling me that I did it to hurt him? How? When? As far as I know, we were done for good; there were no more prospects for us! When I went to have sex with Ted, I never for one minute thought about Patrick: that's how 'DONE' I thought our relationship was. If I'd ever have thought that there was a chance, I would never have sex with another man. Again, whatever. Maybe this time he can learn a lesson on how to be considerate of other people's feelings. He treated my feelings like a disease and now he wants me to feel embarrassed of what I have done because he is hurt? Nah, it's NOT going to happen!'

I was asleep when my phone buzzed around 1 a.m. Patrick sent me a message, basically saying: 'You are a toxic person, you destroy everything that you touch. I cannot teach you anything because you don't listen. Don't ever contact me again, I am sorry about Gabriel, but I cannot help him.'

I read that message twice and I laughed because it sounded ridiculous. Everything he said in the message said more about him than me. I thought about replying and telling him off or saying something nasty to make him more upset. But I did nothing: doing nothing is the best you can do with manipulative people. Plus, I was at peace with myself. If his intentions were to upset me or have me chase him for his forgiveness, he could wait for it in his sleep because I too was done with his nonsense and manipulative ways. I still had no knowledge at this stage that I was dealing with a narcissist. However, I was fully aware that he was selfish, emotionally unavailable, manipulative, arrogant, damaged and mean most of the time when things didn't go his way.

That night I slept like an angel, knowing I had my closure, and I was SUPER ready to close that door and move on! Next morning, I sent the message to Dalila, and she came to my room before leaving for work. She asked me what happened, and after she learned all facts, we both laughed at how entitled he felt in our relationship, about the fact he could date and sleep with people while we were together but felt 'hurt' because I slept with someone after we finished.

She asked me how I was, and I said I was feeling great, that I wanted to distance myself from him for a while but was reluctant because of Gabriel and because I still loved him, but I knew deep inside for so many reasons that it was the right thing to do. She expressed her concern, said she could see the relationship was good for me and Gabriel in a way but that there was something that made her feel uneasy most of the time. She said she never really got very involved because it wasn't her place to do so, but she had her doubts. However, she was really pissed off with the fact he said he loved Gabriel like a son but was ready to dismiss him like an object. He should at least have asked me to bring Gabriel, she said, so he could have a conversation with him and let him know they wouldn't be seeing each other any time soon. I told Dalila I thought the same for a minute, but then felt it was great that I wouldn't have to see his face again. She had to leave for work but said we should open a bottle that night and drink on it.

In the afternoon, I called Gabriel to my room and I said I had something very important to tell him. All the other times me and Patrick finished, I never got Gabriel involved or let him know exactly what was going on. When Patrick finished with me over email, I did say to Gabriel that me and Patrick would just be good friends and he had nothing to worry about. But, this time, I was going to tell him everything, in the best way a child could understand.

I started to say: 'Gabriel, I know you love Uncle Patrick like a dad, but he and mom are not talking now, and he is very upset, and he's asked me not to contact him anymore. That means that you too won't be able to see him. I know this is probably difficult for you to hear, but I want you to understand that it has nothing to do with you. It's grown-up problems and I am really sorry that you have to be affected by it.'

'What did you do to him, for him to be that upset with you?'

'Well, I went out with a male friend after me and Uncle Patrick finished. And I told him two days ago and he felt betrayed about it. He thinks I am a bad person for it!'

'That's not fair! He has loads of friends (female) on his computer. I see him texting them sometimes, so why can't you have friends too?'

My blood started boiling – I knew what Gabriel meant! So, he was having conversations with women online while my son was around? What the hell? But I kept my cool and I said: 'Yes, some people are like that. Anyway, how do you feel about what I just told you? Do you want to ask me anything else?'

'No, I am OK, Mom. I am sad I am not going to see him anymore because he was good to me, but he wasn't very good to you. So, never mind.'

It was like a rock hit me in my chest! So, I asked him: 'What do you mean, he wasn't good to me?'

'I heard him shouting at you sometimes for no reason. You didn't laugh much around him like you do with your friends and he didn't kiss you or hug you like couples do in the movies. I don't think he loved you, Mom, but he had a ring for you though.'

I felt like crying after that. All this time I was trying to make things work for me, but mostly for Gabriel. Trying to stay in a relationship I thought would benefit my son, but he was being damaged by seeing his mother being humiliated by a man. I would always try to be cautious and make sure Gabriel wasn't listening or around when Patrick would have his 'tantrums', but I guess it is true what they say: 'Kids are great observers and listeners!'

I felt so hurt that my son saw me go through all of it, that I didn't protect him from that, and I actually felt angry with myself for that. I hugged Gabriel really tight, and I told him: 'Thank you for understanding, and sorry if I disappointed you in any way, and also sorry you had to see Uncle Patrick showing poor behaviour towards me. I just wanted you to be happy, and I thought that being with him made you happy. From now on, I will always check with you first. I always told you that, but I need you to understand that when I say that you can trust me with anything, it means anything, alright? Next time, please tell Mom what you just told me. That you don't think that person is being good to me and how that makes you feel, alright?'

Straight after, I asked: 'Did he ever do or say anything bad to you that made you feel uncomfortable?'

He told me no, that he was just a little bit impatient sometimes, but was always good to him. I hugged him again and told him that we would be all right, and that I loved him very much. Straight after, he went to play, and I sat on my bed contemplating all I had been through with Patrick, and the way my relationship with him unfolded through those months. I felt stupid and angry with myself for allowing him to control and manipulate me the way he did, to play with my feelings like I was a doll and make me feel less than nothing at times, make me believe I wasn't good enough for him, feel crazy and doubt myself, be incapable of driving my life or being a good mother.

I felt enraged, with him but mostly with myself. I felt like I needed to explore why I let myself go in that way and understand why I was so needy! I could stand up for myself but hated the sense of loneliness or not having someone to love or love me and, most importantly, someone to make me happy. I was so eager for that idea that I let this man do with me whatever he wanted and act up with me as he pleased.

The next time I had therapy with Ian, we discussed all the emotions that was going through my mind. Ian was happy we'd broken up and to see I was out from under Patrick's 'spell'! He was proud of my progress but, of course, we both knew I would need a bit more time to move on completely from Patrick. We discussed my role in the relationship, and in the end, it was obvious to me that, because I didn't love myself enough, I didn't know my true value. Therefore, I wasn't aware of what happiness was: I kept looking for it in friends, men and family. My childhood was so chaotic, so damaging, so painful, so estranged of love that I didn't know who I was, what my purpose and my value was. I knew I was resilient, strong-minded, loyal and a fighter, but also a bomb emotionally. Everything was black and white to me, I was an either 'you-love-me-or-you-hate-me' kind of person. I could say I hated Patrick for all the things he said to me and the way he treated me, but after I started to understand my weaknesses, I owned the fact he acted toward me the way he did to me allowing him to do so. I created an idea/future in my head and I very desperately wanted to live up to that idea. I went into that relationship without boundaries or a firm, strong voice.

For a couple of months after we finished, I was still replaying things in my head, situations that happened where I thought I acted wrongly, still doubting myself, asking if I had acted differently whether things could have been different. Again, I almost drove myself crazy wondering if there was any truth in his mean words and trying to clear up the blurred lines between his craziness, toxicity and evilness against my naivety.

Looking back, I didn't understand that abuse is not just physical. Psychological abuse is real and can leave you scarred for the rest of your life if it's not addressed. I did have a hard time understanding that I did nothing wrong, apart from falling in love with a narcissist. Apparently, that's what happens when you come out of a relationship with a narcissistic person, and that's where therapy came in quite handy.

After I connected all the dots, I hated him with all my guts. He knew exactly what he was doing. He 'gaslighted' me, picked on me, gave me hope with no intention of compromising in our relationship. I hated him and, most of the time, I felt like going there and telling him a few home truths to his face, because he almost destroyed my sanity. But the more I learned about narcissistic people, the more I knew I needed to be away from him; and that helped me come to terms with our relationship and with the psychological abuse I'd endured. Plus, toxic people like Patrick never let things go, can't move forward: they bully and intimidate others, they lie, create drama, play and act out of fear and insecurity, so there was no point in me trying to call him out on anything.

## To Patrick: you can't break what was broken before

I forgave you already! Not because I wanted to, but my reluctance to do so made me stay attached to you for too long! As soon as I understood the narcissist in you, I started looking at you as a monster that needs to be put away, far away from people, because all your kind do is walk around hurting innocent people like me. All I ever wanted was love, to love you and be loved. All you was destroy me mentally. You brought out the inner child in me so many times – the unloved, hurt, lost, guilty and ashamed child. However, in the end, you also brought out the fighter child in me! The same one that didn't take the glass of rat poison and chose to fight against her bullies every day until they left her alone! You tried to 'destroy' me with your evil and twisted ways, but I have known evil before and I rose from that, so I knew that, eventually, I was going to 'rise' from you and that in a heart where God lives, no darkness can prevail!

-    *Narcissist Unmasked* ~

*'Sweetheart stop beating yourself up.*
*The truth is you are a fabulous person.*

*A diamond in a sea of rocks. That asshole you thought you had a future with? Well, that's never going to happen, because he is hopelessly broken inside somewhere. The damage to his soul is never going to mend. There is no room for improvement.*

*The only thing you can do now is know that you dance with the devil, and that given the chance the devil would destroy you completely. You mean nothing to him now.*

*As lonely as it may seem, it's time to wipe the stink off that that asshole left behind in his monster wake; take a good look within and take care of yourself!*

*Unlike him, you can fix what's going on within you.'*

-   *By Brenda Korneder –*


I started writing this chapter thinking that I needed to solely forgive you for all the pain and rage that I felt after I understood the monster in you. But, actually, what I realise is that I need to forgive myself more for the guilt I have for involving myself with you, putting my son in the middle of our relationship, letting you control me, for believing and trusting you blindly, for living a fairy tale in my mind based on the false hopes you were giving me. I forgive myself for allowing you to have so much power over me. I have learned a great lesson with you! I learned to love, trust and always believe in myself. I learned the true power of therapy. I learned to be a better mother for Gabriel through it. As you see, you did teach me something, and I did learn it! I now choose to concentrate on those positive things and feel nothing but love for you (but I still don't like you). Thank you for the hard lessons; they showed me the way through to my happiness.

I forgive you as I forgive myself and I wish you well, especially regarding your mental health.

Here and now, I let you go.

# Chapter 5
## Dalila – 'My right arm'

I met Dalila through Pedro's brother (Miguel), but we only became good friends four years later, and when Pedro left, she became my right arm in everything that concerned Gabriel' schedules. I often tell people I have a job because Dalila was my salvation in a time when I thought my hands were tied. I took the full-time job because she assured me she would help me with Gabriel, and she never failed me. I was in one of the lowest points in my life: struggling to keep a job, maintain a house and being a mother all on my own, and she was my strength through it all. She was more like Gabriel's mom to him than I was during those times. I was overwhelmed and could not function properly at home; I was a good professional, but I had no patience at home to be a mother and with all the responsibilities that come with that. She sat with me so many times and schooled me through it: the importance of making time for Gabriel, for myself and those who loved me.

She told me it was OK to ask for help, that she was happy to help, and I would also help her in whatever way I could. I guess a friendship works like that. I recognise that I put on her more than I should but, looking back, I didn't think about that because my head wasn't in the right space. But I am sure that all the times she needed me, and I was able to help, I also didn't fail her (at least I don't think so). I could be here blaspheming against her, but I won't do that. In fact, I want this to be the shortest chapter of them all!

Me and Dalila fell out in March of 2017. I had an amazing opportunity to go to Disneyland Paris through my company; the package included three adults and four children for three days and two nights, staying at any Disneyland hotel at a very reasonable price. I had other friends asking me about deals like that all the time, but since I also wanted to go, and I knew it was one of Dalila's dreams, I put us as a priority. I then invited another two friends to come with us. In the end, it was only me, Dalila, and her daughter, Gabriel and Maria's daughter, going to Paris.

The trip on the way there was exhausting but good; the kids were in good spirits and super-excited. However, as soon we got to Disney, the dynamic changed, as it was two little girls and my boy. I can understand that: they are girls, and they want to do girl things, he is a boy, and he wants to do boy things. But, as we came together and Gabriel had no one else to play or do things with him, my suggestion as an adult was: let's compromise! We will do things in turns: do boy things and then girl things and vice versa until we get back home. From my point of view, that was only fair, and I expected Dalila to back me up on this.

However, that wasn't the case, and from the beginning Gabriel felt left out and ganged up on, to the point where he asked me if we could go back to Disneyland one day again, but with his mates. Dalila was there, heard what he said, and saw that he was upset. I was upset after seeing the behaviour of the girls, but I chose not to say anything because it was being created by her daughter and I felt that, as a mother, she should be the one calling her daughter out, and telling her they should blend together. If she didn't like being ignored or bullied by her half-brothers, then she shouldn't be doing the same to Gabriel. If Sabrina (Maria's daughter) wasn't there, she would most likely have been mates with Gabriel and wanted to do things with him as usual. Sabrina, I could see, was just following the behaviour of her friend, trying to fit in.

One of the days, we were queuing to see Spider-Man. Her daughter kept moaning that she didn't want to be there, and Dalila still didn't call her out. By that point, I had had enough, so I said to Dalila: 'You know what! You guys go do girls' things and me and my son will do boys' stuff. This was supposed to be a fun time together, but if that is upsetting your daughter having to wait for Gabriel to have his turn doing things, then I think it is best if we split up. Let's meet up for lunch at 1 p.m. in front of Planet Hollywood, as I only have one voucher and we need to be together to claim my employee discount.'

She didn't seem bothered or even to have considered my son's feelings! She just said that perhaps that was the best thing to do and left. Honestly, I am all right doing things on my own, even if on holiday with people, but my son, like any other child, wanted company to share all the experiences and then talk and laugh about that. We stood in the queue and, as they left, Gabriel turned around and said: 'So they don't want to do things with us?'

'They want to go see the princesses and other girl things. If you want, we can go with them. It is up to you, or we can just go and do and see what you want and then meet them for lunch. I am sure we will still have a good time. Gabriel you don't need other people to have fun.'

'I know, Mom, but it's nice to have company. They have each other …'.

'I know babe! But you have me and there is so much to do and see here that you won't even have time to think about them.'

We did have a great time together. That's the thing about Disney: it's a magical place where you can't be mad for too long (so I thought)!

At 1 p.m. we went to meet them at the restaurant. I wasn't in my best mood, just at the thought of having to sit with them. Honestly, I wished, from that point, it was just me and my son, to avoid any more animosity. While we were waiting for the table, Gabriel was trying to fit in with the girls by telling them what he had been doing. Again, Sophie (Dalila's daughter) kept dismissing him and talking over him and pulling Sabrina's attention toward her and away from Gabriel. My son would say something and she would be mean, ignore him or tell him that they weren't interested.

After a while, I had had enough, so I called Gabriel out in front of them: 'Gabriel, do you like to be humiliated? Can't you see that they do not want to talk or play with you? Why do you keep trying to fit in with them? You need to learn that sometimes it is best to be alone than fit in with the mean people that have no regard for your feelings.'

I then turned around to the girls and said (in a very loud and upset tone): 'Sophie, you keep complaining to your mom about your half-brothers bullying and ganging up on you, and now you are doing the same to Gabriel? This was supposed to be a great time together and your behaviour towards him has been poor and mean. Shame on you! Sabrina, you haven't done it so much: but you need to learn that sometimes fitting in is not the best option, especially when the people you are trying to fit in with are being mean to others. Learn to speak for yourself and stand out from the crowd.'

I then picked Gabriel up and went to sit away from them, as I needed a minute to chill. I could see Sophie crying and Dalila trying to calm her down. She then came to me and said: 'Wanuza, there was no need for that! They are kids: they fight one minute, and they are fine the next one. I think you using the words mean and bullying was a bit out of order.'

That was it, my chill was gone! What the HELL! Have you been here with us (I thought)? Then I asked: 'Dalila are you for real? Haven't you noticed the behaviour of your daughter towards Gabriel this whole time?'

'They are like that; they fight and then they are all right,' she said.

'Dalila, they are not fighting! Your daughter is being a complete diva, and because she has Sabrina's company, she's completely shut out Gabriel from any conversations or interactions. You can't see that because she is happy and having a great time, but my son is feeling left out, and for your information, he felt sad and disappointed that you guys went your way, and he was left alone with me. She had someone to share with and to talk to, who does he have? Gabriel, do you mind telling Auntie Dalila how you feel about the whole experience, so she doesn't think that your mom is overreacting?'

'I wish I could have come with my mate Christian or Jeremiah because the girls are being mean to me,' Gabriel said. 'They don't want to talk, play or do things with me, and when we are in our room, they say mean things to me and then they laugh at me.'

'There you go! You are always talking about your step kids, how that makes you feel and how it affects your child. I brought my son here to have a good time, not to be feeling like this. And you know what really pisses me off? I expected more from you. The whole time, I was waiting for you to call your daughter out for her behaviour: first, because it is not acceptable and, second, you are like a second mother to Gabriel, so I expected more from you. But no, you stayed quiet the whole time, and the only time you decided to talk was when I called her out for her behaviour. Nah, I am not having it, Dalila. No one attacks my son, makes him feel shit and gets away with that. NO ONE. Not even another child. I have been bullied before; I know how it feels. I waited for you to say something, and you didn't: that says more about you than me!' I was shouting at her.

Dalila turned to Gabriel and said: 'Gabriel, I am sorry. Auntie doesn't want you feeling that way. From now on we will do things together. Girls, please apologise to him!'

They said sorry, but I said to stop it as I could see they didn't mean it. After that, we had lunch in the most awkward silence ever. Dalila then asked me if I was going to continue to be upset with her, and I said I needed time to chill. We then went to see the Star Wars showcase that me and Gabriel had scheduled for 3 p.m. I wasn't expecting them to come with us, but they came.

I was ready to just let go of what happened and start all over again, but again her daughter started pulling faces, as she wasn't impressed with the show and that's not what she wanted to do. From that point on I was very clear: 'Dalila, do whatever you want with the girls. I honestly do not want you guys with us; we will be fine on our own. Let's just meet for meals and that's it.'

Of course, after all that was said, Dalila chose to follow us around with the girls, which made things even worse, because it annoyed me even more.

**The betrayal:** *'Only those you trust can betray you!'*
 - *Terry Goodkind* –

We returned to the UK and, for weeks we didn't really talk much to each other. I knew we had to sit and talk about what went down in Paris, but I was still upset, and I didn't want to talk to her out of rage and make things worse. Things were awkward, as she was the one still taking Gabriel to school and picking him up. However, I felt uncomfortable about that after we came back from the holidays and I let her know that I was looking for a childminder for Gabriel. It made perfect sense, as she wasn't living with us anymore, and was starting a new life with her new man. I thought that was the best time for me to become 'independent' regarding Gabriel. Depending on other people to stay with him was always something that annoyed me, but no one is that self-independent that they don't need help from other people, and I was no exception to the rule. I spoke to my manager, and she gave me the option of working from home two days a week. The other days I could do 9 a.m. – 3 p.m. in the office and then log on at night to finish my hours. That made my life easy: now I could take and pick up Gabriel from school and take him to his activities in the afternoon without having to depend on Dalila or anyone else (except on special occasions). I informed Dalila of my new arrangements and asked her if it was still OK for her to be my emergency contact and she said yes.

However, after that, we distanced from each other. We went weeks without talking or seeing each other. In the back of my mind, she was always there and we needed to address what happened, but Dalila doesn't like confrontation and I was waiting for the right time.

After weeks without seeing each other we finally met at Catarina son's birthday party. It was a bit awkward in the beginning, but then we just started talking and laughing and, although there was still an elephant in the room, I felt we were both trying to just find out what was going on in each other's lives since we'd last seen each other. She said: 'You will never guess who I have been talking to!'

I thought, Pedro maybe! But I waited for her to tell me.

'Patrick! I came across his number a few weeks ago and I texted him just to see how he was. And then he called me, and we have been talking now and then.'

It was like someone punched me in my stomach! Why the hell was Dalila talking with Patrick? What did she possibly have to say to him? I tried to act cool, but I think it was transparent in my face that it bothered me. So, she asked me: 'It doesn't bother you me talking to him, does it?'

I wanted to laugh at her question. Why was she asking me that now? She should have asked me this before she started texting him. So, I told her it was fine, as long the their conversations wasn't me!

'Well, he did ask about Gabriel and you, of course. But I didn't extend the conversation in that area and I made it clear that if he wanted to be my friend, talking about you was off-limits.'

For some reason, I didn't believe her. My gut distrusted her right there and, from that moment, I felt I should be careful with her. Instantly, the friend I once trusted with mine and my son's life became a stranger. I was looking at her and listening to her telling me the reasons why she called him, but I couldn't believe one word coming out of her mouth.

After a minute, I cut her off and told her: 'Dalila, I don't want to know anything about Patrick! I already told his housekeeper that too. Please don't go share things about my life with him and please don't bring him into my life or make comments regarding him around Gabriel. We are both trying to move on from Patrick. Whatever relationship you guys are trying to establish between you, it's not my business.'

'I am not trying to establish any relationship with him! You are my friend, not him, so don't worry. I am just letting you know so you don't find out from other people.'

I thought, what other people? You are just trying to see what my reaction would be. I hurt you with what I said in Paris and, instead of sitting with me like a good friend to my 'enemy' because you knew that would hurt me equally. But, at the same time, she was my friend: we'd been through so many things together, she helped me so many times, and vice versa. She and her daughter lived with me for almost a year. We shared so much together; I couldn't let Patrick come between us!

I knew Patrick, and his evil ways, so I figured out this was his way of getting back at me, by being friendly with Dalila or even diverging her friendship from me to him. He knew I depended on Dalila greatly, and if I didn't have her, I would be stuck (as I'd said that to him many times).

So, I gave Dalila the benefit of the doubt and told her to be careful with Patrick, as he had a way of twisting things for his own benefit, and I left it there. I didn't think I had to tell her anything else. I'd given her Patrick's number and she was entitled to talk to whoever she wanted, even if I didn't like that person. Also, I'd stressed to her so many times that she should connect with Patrick to help her look for job opportunities. He had good connections and she really needed some encouragement and some money. Perhaps that was her motive, her way to move forward so I tried not to make it about me.

Nevertheless, my gut was 100 per cent disturbed every time I was around her from that point on. I would watch my words and avoid being with her at all costs. I spoke with my friend Elizabete, and she straight away said it was disrespectful and that a good friend would never do that. She knew what happened in Paris because she was the only person I told at the time, and she said it wasn't enough reason to go to my ex and try to be friends with him. That it didn't make any sense. She said that, if she was looking for new job opportunities, she should have done that while we were still together! It made sense, what Beta was saying, and I knew that deep down. But, again, I thought that was the work of the devil (Patrick), and I wasn't going to let him win.

I kept my distance from Dalila. I would still see her occasionally, text her and vice versa, but wouldn't share as much as before. We stayed in this dance for a year. During that year, I tried to observe more instead of talking. I tried not to talk badly about her, not about Paris, her friendship with Patrick, and the fact that she still owned me money from the trip. I didn't say anything to anyone apart from Beta (I knew Beta wouldn't tell anyone). When people asked me about her, I would just say we were both so busy that we hadn't had time to be together.

By doing so, people's truths started coming to me. One of them was Maria. We were in Bournemouth for the weekend at Beta's house. At the end of the second night, we were all a bit tipsy, and the subject of conversation was loyalty and friendship. I remember saying that from the moment a friend broke my trust, it was hard for me to go back to the same place and, funnily enough, I was feeling like that with Dalila. Something had told me to not trust her like I used to.

Maria then said I was right and that I shouldn't trust her. She disclosed everything that happened after Paris. She said Dalila went to her a week after and told her about the argument we had. She probably thought me, or Sabrina had already told her what happened. When Maria said she didn't know, she then started saying she was so distressed when she came back that she didn't know what to do or what to say, so she called Patrick for some guidance. Maria said she felt uncomfortable knowing that, because she knew we didn't finish on good terms, so what would Patrick have to say about it that would help the situation?

Maria refused to repeat everything that Dalila had told her, but she did say: 'Wanuza, she could have come to any of us for comfort and advice because we know you exactly as you are; but she chose Patrick because he would validate whatever bad thoughts she was having against you. She knew exactly what she was doing. She tried to justify her behaviour with me. I listened to her and did agree that you have a short temper sometimes, but I told her that as you'd been friends for so long she should be trying to resolve things with you.'

My gut was right all along. She did go to my 'enemy' to get an ally out of him. I know she didn't really know everything that went down between me and Patrick, but she was present through all of our relationship and she saw how it affected me at times, so how could she do that to me, betray me like that? I looked at Beta across the table and all I heard was: 'I never trusted that bitch! There was always something about her that I didn't like!'

Funnily enough, my mother and my friend Tuxa had never been fond of Dalila either. But I guess, because she was always there for me and I was always talking wonders about her, they ended up tolerating her.

When I got back to Wolverhampton, I thought about calling Dalila to have a conversation, but I didn't want to put Maria on the spot, so I delayed it for weeks. One day, Dalila showed up at my door unexpectedly and I couldn't hide my displeasure at seeing her. I was working from home, so I made an excuse that I was really busy. I know she felt uncomfortable, as she didn't stay long. She texted me in the evening, apologising for coming around without asking in advance but, that as she was in the areas, she just wanted to drop my travel bag back and catch up with me. I didn't feel like pretending anymore, so I told her why I wasn't pleased to see her:

'After I know that you felt the need to call Patrick to talk about our argument, I decided to forget about the luggage, the money and you! I believe you had your reasons, but coming from you, who followed my relationship with him and was happy when we finished, it makes me question your reasons... a real friend would never do that to me, regardless of being upset with me. Anyway, thank you for everything you ever did for me and Gabriel but, unfortunately, I will also never forget the knife that you stuck into my back.'

Just like Patrick used to do, she tried to turn it against me: 'No, you should know that there are always two sides to any story. Nowadays, I don't care about being right or explaining myself to anyone. If that is how you feel than I can only wish all the best to both of you. Kisses.'

Straight after that she sent me another message: 'Ah, I also heard things from Patrick and from other people about me that could only have come from you. But a monkey only looks at another monkey's ass (Portuguese proverbs) and it is very hypocritical of you. People should evaluate themselves before judging other people.'

I knew this dance, and I wasn't willing to enjoy the music or entertain a back-and-forwards string of messages, so I just responded: 'You are right Dalila; you are very right!'

I blocked her number on my phone, Facebook and messenger! All I needed was for her to own her stuff and maybe we could sit and talk through our differences. But I knew Dalila, and that is the reason I chose to text her instead of asking directly to her face. I knew that when she feels trapped, she goes around and around talking about her problems and, in the end, you come out of the conversation feeling guilty and stupid for even confronting her. I knew I wasn't getting anywhere with her. There and then, we had nothing else to talk about. Nothing else that wasn't the truth. She wasn't ready to address it and I wasn't willing to be manipulated by her or anyone else again in my life.

## To Dalila: I can't let you go yet... but I forgive you

I know I was out of order in Paris and I do apologise that we've never had this conversation before. Before I lashed out, I should have told you privately how Gabriel was feeling and asked you to have a conversation with your daughter. Looking back, it was immature of me; I was the adult (and you) and I should have known better. I know the fact I was bullied at school played a big role in that argument: anything that brought me close to my past or my bad feelings always set me on fire instantly. Seeing my son feeling bullied and sad made me feel really upset with the situation and act in a bad way. I apologise for that. I apologise for shouting at you and your daughter and acting childishly throughout the process. I apologise for not apologising to you before you felt the urge to go to Patrick. I especially apologise for not letting you know the REAL Patrick and what I have been through with him. However, a good friend of mine didn't need to know all the details to know that doing what you have done is a betrayal. In anyone else's thinking, it would make more sense if you had gone to Pedro, as you know him way better than Patrick. And, if you really wanted to talk with someone that knew me as you do, you could have gone to Beta, Tuxa, Catarina or Maria? Why Patrick? It wasn't an accident! You knew his opinion of me: he told you before!

Like Maria said, you needed to have your bad thoughts of me validated and Patrick was the only one, or the best option. I hope he gave you the comfort you needed; I hope that sacrificing our friendship over Patrick's false truths of me was worth it. I've forgiven you for that already though and, very honestly, I don't hold any grudges against you. I still love you and your daughter, and I still think about you both at times. I still worry and I still care. We have a lot of history and we could actually move past all of this and be friends again; I've thought about it many times, but I can't trust you anymore, and I can't look at your face and not be cynical.

You were once my right arm, my confidant, my sister, my everything when it came to Gabriel. I expected betrayal from so many people, but I never saw it coming from you. If your intention was to hurt me, congratulations, you achieved it. Don't worry, I haven't been blaspheming you around others! Like I said, I still love you and I will NEVER forget everything that you have done for us, and for that same reason I choose not to speak about you in a spiteful way. I am here only talking my truth and my version of the events that hurt me and which I need closure from. I will never put you down amongst people or continue to resent you for what happened. I want to move forward and believe that maybe one day, when we are old, we can sit down, have a glass of wine (or tea) and laugh about the past. But, right now, all I can do is forgive you your poor choice and forgive myself for not being capable of addressing our issues there and then.

I also acknowledge that this time I have been away from you has been good for my self-growth as a mother, woman and friend. I've realised that relying on you had its benefits, but also its disadvantages, and since then I have been on a learning curve. I don't think I am ready to let you go (because I still have hope for us), but I wish you well and success always, and be assured that if tomorrow you need me, I will still be there for you regardless …

I just cannot be your friend right now!  Thank you for always being there It meant and still means a lot to me.

# Chapter 6
## Gabriel – 'My Angel, my Root of strength'

'Heaven on earth is looking at my little boy!'
- Jenny McCarthy –

My son, you are the love of my life, my strength and my joy!
I dreamed of you before I had you; I knew God was going
to give me the boy I always wanted, and I knew that
you were going to change my life for the better.

We had a bumpy start from the time you were born until
the age of three, when your father left. I remember the day
of your arrival: I was in labour for thirty-two hours. It was
horrible and painful, but as soon as I saw your little face,
my heart stopped. The love I felt for you was so
overwhelming that I started crying. I never felt anything
like that before. I felt like I couldn't breathe, I couldn't take
my eyes off you and I wanted to hold you the entire time.
However, we didn't have much time to bond during the
two nights we spent in the hospital or when we went back
home. In the hospital, I was losing too much blood and
they took you from me because I needed a blood
transfusion. At home I had a chest infection and the doctor
prescribed me penicillin, which made my milk dry, so I
couldn't breastfeed you. My milk was already weak, and

the medication dried it completely. You had to go straight to formula, and because I was in constant pain from the surgery and the infection, your dad and my mother would take you from the room in the morning to let me rest, and only bring you in the afternoon for your bath and some time with me. That was our routine for a week. It's safe to say that created a gap between you and me. After that week, I didn't 'recognise' you as my baby anymore. Your crying annoyed me, and I didn't want to do anything that related to you like bath, change your nappy, feed you or even play with you. You were a sweet and calm baby, but you weren't 'mine' anymore: something changed, and I couldn't explain what. My love for you was still there, and I would look at you and smile and think 'how cute is he?', but then again, I am like that with any other child. Looking back, I think my postpartum depression started right there, but never was addressed.

From that tender age, your bond was always more with your dad. He was the one waking up at night to feed you, the one always more patient with you, always willing to play and do things with you. I was all right about not getting very involved; I knew, and I embraced my obligations to you, but I was always happy to let him or anyone else take over. I loved you as my child and always felt very protective of you, but at the same time I didn't know how to 'show' you love. Every time you would reach out for me, I would panic inside, not knowing what to do! I was always jealous of how natural it was for your dad to bond and deal with you. I used to sit down and observe you both, and my joy would come from that.

I remember, two weeks after I had you, my mother had to go back to Portugal and your dad went back to university and work. I know your grandmother was worried about letting me stay home alone with you: she could see I wasn't myself. But your dad probably thought I was just being lazy and wanted to stay in bed all day.

The first time I found myself alone with you at home, my heart started racing. Everything was all right while you were sleeping, but then you woke up and after I fed you and changed your nappy, you cried continuously. I tried to calm you down, but it was useless, so after a while I was so exhausted and stressed that I too started crying. I didn't know what else to do, so I put you back in your Moses basket, closed the living room door and sat on the kitchen floor crying and covering my ears. I don't remember how long I stayed there for: all I recall is your dad coming home, opening the kitchen door, looking at me puzzled and then closing it again and reaching out for you. He never asked me what happened or if I was OK, never made an argument out of it, he just completely ignored what had happened, and I also pretended that it was just a bad dream.

Later that day, he told me you had colic and the crying was from that and he showed me what to do. When the midwife came after a few days, she asked me how I was feeling, and I tried to acknowledge what happened, but your dad cut the conversation off by asking something about baby formulas and colic. I asked him later that day why he did that? He said that in this country we risked losing you to the system.

I knew I needed some help, that I was experiencing some kind of depression, but we were told that midwifes could take you away if we didn't seem fit to raise you; and losing you was never an option. So, I dealt with it on my own. I was used to getting out of a dark hole on my own – I have done it before – and I knew it was imperative to do so then. Your dad was great in the sense that he took over most of the obligations regarding you and told me to join the gym, and even started supporting me with my university things, because he saw that they were things that made me happy and, when I came home, I was a different person: happy, joyful and loving.

Just like my mother, I realised very early I wasn't stay-at-home-mother (wife) material. That had nothing to do with the love I felt for you, it just meant that I was a better mother and person while doing my own 'thing'.

When your father left, the thought of being at home full-time taking care of you and the house, drove me nuts. I think God knew that would have been my slow death, and therefore he presented me with the opportunity to work at a company that was an answer to my prayers. However, I was so focused on keeping the job and proving to them and to the world that I was a single mother but could do it all, that I forgot the most important thing: you!

I threw myself into work and didn't deal with my resentment of your father leaving. I knew I didn't love him anymore, but from the moment we had you, I thought we were a team. Work was my escape from reality, from bills, from being a single mother, from dealing with my emotions, from the household obligations and from you! As long I was busy with work, I didn't have to deal with any of it, including you, or perhaps acknowledging that you needed me.

Auntie Dalila was crucial during this time, as you would be with her most times and would prefer to be there to home. She didn't seem to mind, you looked happy and I was relieved that someone was there for you, because I couldn't be, and I knew it. I knew you needed me, your mother, my love. The fact is, I needed myself, time to heal, knowledge, love. You can only give what you have inside, and at the time I had nothing: I was numb and in auto mode, trying my best to survive and keep going one day after another.

I was always angry, always upset with everything and everyone. I was a miserable person at home and with you, but with fake smiles for others and at work. I was so self-absorbed that I failed to understand you too were hurting. I didn't love your father anymore, but you did, and you do! I failed to understand that you 'lost' your father and your mate, the one that used to take you to the park every time you asked, play football with you, the one that rolled over on the floor with you and played with you for hours without complaining he was tired or that he had work to do. You 'lost' him and became an 'orphan' because I neglected you physically and emotionally. I praise Auntie Dalila and Nana Flora because they helped me, especially with you, in a time that I failed to help you and myself. I remember always feeling so annoyed every time I had to spend too much time with you, dealing with your tantrums and your childish behaviour. All the motherhood obligations irritated me so much, especially on the weekends, when all I wanted to do was to stay in bed all day and forget about the outside world. As sad as it might sound, sometimes I felt you were like a curse that your dad left behind to remind me of him and for the fact I never really loved him as much as he loved me. I never felt the urge to hurt you or do something bad to you but, most of the time, I wondered how my life would be if your dad came and took you away.

The turning point of our estranged relationship happened when you started school. You were so excited to start, but after a few weeks I noticed your excitement faded away. When I went to the first parent evening at school, I understood why. Your teacher said you were behind in class and reading was a struggle for you, that you were good with numbers but would get overwhelmed every time you had to read. When I asked why, you said because all the other kids were ahead of you and would make fun of you: that would make you nervous and make you cry. I looked at the teacher, hoping for some understanding; but all I had from her was: 'I understand all of that, but he needs to get over that! However, given his background and circumstances as a family, I think he is progressing in steady steps. He just needs a little push at home to help him keep up.'

I was confused with what she said, so I asked: 'What do you mean by that!'

'No disrespect, but it came to my attention that you work full-time and Gabriel spends most of his time in childcare. I also know that you are a single parent, living in a foreign country with no family around. It could be worse: he is a bright child, and he is coming around but, of course, our expectations for him are not high, so as not to pressurise him.'

I could not believe what I'd just heard. I was beyond furious, but I showed no reaction. Instead, I said thank you for your time and we left. We sat in the car for a while and I started crying. I am not sure if you saw me as I tried my best to hide it. Again, at night on my bed, I let myself go. Who was she to put you in the 'social misconception bag'? How dare she label you? Yes I work a lot, Yes, you come from a single-parent household. Yes, you live on a council estate. SO WHAT?! Barack Obama, was raised in a single parent household and he became the first black president of America.

I was so infuriated, in that moment I decided you wouldn't be a government statistic. You are my son and I know you are as bright and resilient as I am, and I wasn't going to allow anyone, I mean NO one, to discriminate against you because of our circumstances. I learned a long time ago that all a child needs sometimes is ONE adult to care for them, to guide them, assure them of their capabilities, teach and protect them.

The next day I went to work, and I spoke with both my managers. I told them that although I needed the money, I would have to start working part-time because you needed me. They knew my struggles, because I was always open with them about it, so they suggested I do flexible hours, working two days from home. Eventually, after my fallout with Auntie Dalila, I become more present by working 9 a.m. – 3 p.m. and flexible hours here and there. I felt like crying: I was overwhelmed with their compassion and understanding. I know as managers they were probably just managing personnel and damage control on the team; but their compassion meant and means a lot still, and for that I will always be grateful to them.

The week after we started our new routine, things began to change. There was no more dropping you at 7 a.m. at the childminder and picking you up from there at 4 p.m. I also started to read books regarding child psychology, how to help children with self-confidence, how to discipline without hurting or damaging your children, helping children find their own voice, and about children's mental health. All the books around those subjects agreed that the basis of everything is love, that the love language of children is 'TIME': quality time you spend with them, doing things and building memories. I was coming around with my own self-love, I was also more open to giving more of it to you, and that was the main root of all the changes between me and you. I also read a book regarding single mothers raising boys; that helped me understand I was capable of raising you. Until then, I never thought I was capable of raising you properly, because you were a boy and I a woman. For me, you needed your dad: that should be his obligation not mine – boys need a man to teach them to be a man, so what could I teach you? What kind of a man would come from you growing up with a woman, and a broken woman at that point? I realised then that my resentment towards your dad was all around that. He left me with the burden of that responsibility. What if I failed? What if you became a drug addict? A criminal? A horrible human being? It would always be my fault because I didn't know how to raise a boy and all the complexities that boys have that I do not understand.

However, through my readings, I understood I didn't need to know how to raise a boy or a girl: all I needed to know was how to raise a human being! To teach you compassion, humility, love, forgiveness, integrity, hard work, respect, loyalty and self-love and care. However, I needed to make sure I was surrounded by strong male figures that could be your role models and pass on to you good examples of how to be a great and respectful, hard-working man, not only for me, but for yourself and for the world.

That's when I enrolled you in karate. You needed something out of school (Patrick 's suggestion) that would help with your self-confidence, shyness, help you find your own voice and learn to shut down the outside voices that used to make you doubt yourself. You hated me for that, used to cry every time you had to go to karate, but I had to put my foot down because, slowly, I started seeing the changes in you, and even the teacher that once had few expectations for you was now complimenting you on your fast progress. Karate was slowly taking your inhibitions and fears away and was building you up brick by brick. Look at you now, a chatterbox, funny and with too much voice at times (laugh). I loved it though! I love it when you think I am being unfair and negotiate until you get what you want, or when you talk back because you think that I am talking without all the facts. I love it that you tell me it as it is, with no sugar coating, no pretending. Things are as they are, and if you learn it now, you then know how to deal with frustration. I love it when I ask you if I am fat and sometimes you say yes and then say: 'Maybe you shouldn't have eaten that cake yesterday (laugh)!' I love it that you speak up about everything (even when it is nothing to do with you): it shows me that you have a voice, and you are not afraid of using it.

Uncle Patrick wasn't the best man for me, but I must acknowledge that he was fulcra during this process. He noticed from the beginning my relationship with you wasn't healthy and started giving me books to read and talking to me about parenthood, depression and therapy. Things started to change while I was with him and, today, they are much, much better. It's just a shame I didn't realise soon enough I didn't need to have a man at home to teach you how to be one. That would have saved me and you all the hassle and heartbreak my relationship with him brought to us. I never understood why so many women stay in abusive relationship, but I can now: if you don't believe in your capabilities, the prospect of a better life is nothing but a distant dream, and in the end, I was really trying to make it work for you (but it's not your fault at all).

We have a good life now. I work hard so that we can enjoy life by travelling and making memories together! We have good people in our lives. I made sure I built a good network of people around you and me so that they could jump in during emergencies or just to be our family in the UK. I am in a new and healthy relationship with a man that respects and loves me as I am, that understands I am a mother first and is willing to help me raise you without overstepping or being overbearing with me. I know it was difficult for you to accept him in the beginning. I remember the day I told you I was dating Stennett, and you told me you didn't like him. I knew it was a jealousy thing because you adored him previously. The weeks after that were challenging: we were in constant conflict over everything – your behaviour was off the rails and I had a meltdown. On that day I lost my patience with you, and I smacked you. After that I remember your words: 'I hate you. You don't love me anymore: you just care about Stennett now!'

That made me understand your fears straight away. I called your school and asked them if they could provide counselling for you because you were struggling to overcome the fear of losing me. Instead of telling me your fear, you were misbehaving, being rude to Stennett and to me, being ungrateful and unkind. That is NOT you! Once again, all you needed was to be reassured that I love you and nothing and NO one (I mean NO one) can ever change that. It's nice to see now the bond you have with Stennett and his children; that reassures me that this time I am doing the right thing, and the right thing is to put you first, always!

My little pumpkin, meu filho querido! Before, I saw you as a curse. I had to get out of bed to feed you or to take you to the park. All I wanted was to stay in bed all day, do nothing and think nothing, just redeem myself to my own 'insignificance'.

Today, I see you as my main blessing. You kept me alive during those times, 'obligated' me to keep moving and to evolve. It's safe to say my job kept me sane and you kept me alive!

Today, I find myself many times thinking of when I was less of a mother to you – when I was angry, impatient and empty of emotions toward you – and I feel guilty and ashamed. I can' comprehend now our dynamic then, but that doesn't diminish my guilt. Sometimes, I watch you sleep, and I cry for those times. Sometimes, I hug you tight and you complain that you can't breathe (laughs) or kiss you until you get annoyed. It's just my way of compensating for the love I didn't give you before. I know I can't go back in time, but I am making sure the future is nothing like the past. The way of doing that is taking care of me, because if I am mentally and physically healthy and happy, I function better and can be the mother you deserve to have.

I have nothing to forgive you for because you are just a child, even when you are being naughty! But I can't complain much because you are an excellent son: caring, loving, respectful, extra-super-happy, always excited about things, an A grade student, and it's flattering to have people always praising you for your good manners and kindness. I pray to God you don't ever lose your ways and that, whatever problems you encounter in life, you are self-assured that I am your best friend in life and, although I might get upset, I will always be here for you.

I try to set you good examples every day, because I believe in 'showing' more than 'talking'. I show you the value of working hard and being consistent by taking you on holidays and being able to give you a home and put food on our table every day, the importance of taking care of yourself by eating healthily and through exercise, because that makes me feel good. I show you Love by loving you and putting you first always. I show you kindness by talking with homeless men on the street and buying them food, giving them money or just stop and talking to them. I show you respect and consideration by giving it back to you regardless of you being a child. Sometimes I doubt myself, and ask if I am doing a good job, but other days you reassure me of it by saying: 'Mom, you are the kindest person I know,' or 'Mom, you are a good person!' That warms my heart, although every time I ask you why you are saying it, you just say: 'because you are...' (laugh).

I love you to the moon and back and I hope that one day I can have your forgiveness for the times I was less of a mother to you. Until then, I am trying my best to forgive myself for those times when I didn't know better, where I needed help but did not ask for it! Until then, I will continue to work on myself because of you, more than anyone deserve the best version of myself, and I will continue to hug and kiss you until you get tired of me (laugh).

Thank you for being a good son to me. Your beautiful smile reminds me every day that love is simple and genuine, because all that comes from God is pure. *'Every good and perfect gift is from above, coming down from the father of the heavenly lights, who does not change like shifting shadows.' – James 1:17*

# About Author

My name is Aurea Wanuza Marques Reis, my friends and family call me *Wanuza*. At work or school, I am known as Aurea, as you will have noticed in this book.

I was born in Luanda (Angola) and permanently moved to Portugal in 1992 when I was eleven years old due to the conflicts starting because of political elections. The last time I went there was in 1997, so there is not much I remember from my birth country. I embrace both of my backgrounds because they built me as person. I am 39 now, and I moved to the UK in 2008 when recession hit Portugal really hard.

I am a single mother of a Ten-year-old boy. I graduated from the University College Birmingham in Tourism Business Management and I worked in the sector for six years until I was made redundant due to Covid 19. Currently, I am pursuing a career as a care worker because while writing this book I discovered my caring side, by healing my inner child.

I have discovered my path and I am enjoying pursuing it. My hobbies are writing, fitness, quiet time alone, and spending quality time with close friends and family. My name Aurea comes from the old Latin 'Aurum' and it means something made of gold, golden, that shines.

# I Am Aurea Reis

Little me got scared inside of me for 37 years, she screamed, she cried but the adult me ignored her every plea...

who is she to dare to come out?

who is she to dare to be noticed?

Who is she to dare to try to be loved?

Who is she to try to be heard?

No one cared when your body was being abused by that evil men,

No one cared to ask you about your feelings,

No one cared to show you love,

No one cared to ask you if they could cut down your unapologetic Afro,

No one cared to save you from the white bullies that called you and treated you as a Monkey...

The adult me had to shut you down and embrace your insignificance!

She had to learn to navigate through life with all the rage, pain, frustrations, and sadness of being a woman, black and African.

She learned to fight for anything and against everyone,

Everything was a discussion followed by inexplicable rage!

Dare anyone to defy me,

Dare anyone to try to control or mould me, I would kill them with my mean words and bury them with my nasty attitude.

But I must give it to you little girl, your persistence in coming out and to have a voice, brought me close to God.

You dared to be seen and heard, and I finally let you come out…through tears and sadness… but, you did come out…

The father from the above has been guiding us and I now feel at peace with the tormented feelings I carried around for so long.

You dared to tell me who you are… and Today, I know you!

you are me and I am you, we are woman, black, African, mother, daughter, sister, friend, girlfriend and a daughter of God!

We are valid, our feelings are valid, we are enough, we are loved, our body is respected, but…unfortunately, our black skin is still discriminated every day.

Nevertheless, we now have a voice and we are not afraid of using it!

So, little girl, keep daring, keep pushing and keep being brave and resilient.

I promise to Love you and to continuously let the Above work on us!

You are Aurea Reis and so, Am I…Let's. Never. Forget. It.!

www.marciampublishing.com

Printed in Great Britain
by Amazon

82649438R00130